THE STRATEGY GUIDE FOR PASSING
YOUR BAR EXAM WITH GREATER CONFIDENCE,
IN LESS TIME, AND WITH LESS STRESS THAN THE REST

THE 7 STEPS TO BAR EXAM SUCCESS

DUSTIN SAIIDI, ESQ.

ISBN: 978-0-9892174-0-8

Cover Design: Roland Ali Pantin

To contact Dustin, email:

Dustin@IPassedMyBarExam.com

Facebook.com/IPassedMyBarExam
Twitter: @IPassedmyBarExa

Why You Need To Read This Book

Three weeks into my bar exam prep, I found myself in the shower crying because I did not think I could do it. I did not feel like I was learning the material and my bar exam practice scores were beyond failing.

In December, I had just completed a law school career that put me in the bottom half of my class. According to the statistics provided by our law school, based on my class rank, I had about a 1 in 3 chance of passing the bar exam. To make matters worse, I had already failed the MPRE on my first attempt. I would be taking a good bar prep course, but even they did not focus on helping me improve my writing scores, which were some of my worst grades. And to top it all off, the February bar exam I was going into consistently failed 60% of its takers.

Life was looking dismal.

But, our deepest moments of pain often tend to be the greatest gifts. The pain and struggle I went through forced me to really think about my study approach and revise my strategy. I realized my current approach to bar preparation was highly ineffective. I was wasting a lot of time, expending copious amounts of precious mental energy, and not seeing any improvement in results.

After my 'moment,' I revised my approach into a new system that saved me dozens of hours of time, stress, and headache and made me significantly more prepared than I would have been.

I figured out the strategy of approach that was best suited for the bar exam. I discovered the tactics and methods of study that really made the difference. I learned how to use the power of my mind and body to build my confidence, increase my motivation, and maintain my energy and composure. In less than four months, those tears of pain would turn to tears of joy as I read the beautiful words:

"This name appears on the pass list"

After passing, I began sharing my bar exam success secrets with others. I shared with my friends, then readers of my blog, and now clients that I coach. Dozens of thousands of people have now read, used, and implemented the same techniques to pass the bar exam and did so in a manner that also helped them reduce the amount of time, stress, and headache.

It is time for me to share these same strategies with you.

This book is for bar exam takers looking for the most effective approach to pass and do so with more confidence, peace, and ease along the way. It is for bar exam takers who want to decrease the overwhelming stress and anxiety that comes along with the bar exam.

It is for those who hit that mental block and do not know how to get through it. It is for those who are stressed with acting out of fear of failure and want to study in the peaceful expectation of success. It is for the first-time takers who are looking for the right approach to studying for them. It is for the repeaters who do not want to go through the feeling of failure again.

You have three obstacles that keep you from passing the bar exam:

1. You are not studying the right content.

The bar exam prep programs give you a vast amount of material to study and memorize. But, what they do not tell you is that only a portion of this material needs to be studied for you to do well. In fact, if you aim to study all the material, you *decrease* your chance of success because of the sheer overwhelm, lack of time, and brain capacity to remember it all. The key is to study the content that the graders consistently test on in each topic.

2. You are not using the most effective preparation strategies.

The biggest myth about the bar exam is that you should spend most of your time memorizing rules and learning the law. This is *wrong*! Rules only give you 20% to 30% of the points you will receive on the essays and zero points on your MBE and PT's.

Also, simply reading over and memorizing hundreds of rules on the bar exam is a big waste of time because your brain is not designed for rote memorization. Instead, spend most of your time taking practice tests to learn rules and how the law works in the context of the practice exams. If you do that, you will save a lot of time and become a lot more prepared than the average test taker out there.

3. Your beliefs are not in-sync with a bar exam passer.

If you believe you can do it, you will. If you do not, you will not. It was Gandhi who said something to the effect of:

> Our Beliefs drive our Thoughts
> Our Thoughts drive our Actions
> Our Actions determine our Results

Your thoughts are driven by what is stored in your subconscious mind. Your source of anxiety, fear, and frustration are all rooted in what you allow into your mind on a day-to-day basis. To become effective and pass the bar exam, it is time to be proactive about what message units you place into your brain.

My bar exam strategy will save you time, stress, and headache. It will help you be better prepared to take and pass the bar exam from both a tactical and a mindset perspective. I know because my friends, my clients, and dozens of thousands of readers and podcast listeners have used the same strategies to become bar exam passers.

Before we get started, I would like to make one simple request to you.

Believe in yourself. Believe you can do it. If I can pass the bar exam, so can you. And it starts with that belief.

Introduction

Pass Your Bar Exam in Less Time, With Less Stress, and With More Confidence.

I know I am making a very bold promise in this book. I am claiming you can prepare for your bar exam in fewer hours, with less stress, and with more confidence than most people. And yes, still pass!

In this book, I am going to give you access to that world. I know it is possible for a very good reason. I did it!

I believe I spent fewer hours than most people do in preparing for their bar exam. I took frequent breaks, and I even took off four days in a row a mere three weeks out from test day! I minimized my stress and remained level headed both through the bar prep and during the exam. And, I never even drank a cup of coffee!

There is a problem with the bar exam process. It is filled with false myths.

For example, there is the myth that we have to study long hours in order to pass. Or the myth that we need to start months ahead of our bar prep program start date. You may have been told by your peers that the bar exam is like 12 finals slammed into one long test creating the myth that you need to memorize an extravagant number of rules.

There is the myth that you need to have great, in-depth analysis to impress the graders. Or how about the untruths regarding low pass percentages and who they really apply to. I will tell you why you shouldn't compare yourself to the state average. It is much more involved than that.

Further, people are never taught, during the bar exam or otherwise, anything about the importance of self-image and managing their thoughts, beliefs, body, and energy. Yet, this might be one of the most important things you do to prepare. Without it, you may have added anxiety and never discover the reason for it.

What we have learned about neuroscience in the last five years has been more than what we've learned in the prior 75 years combined! Let us work together to apply this brain science to your bar exam.

I have received incredible feedback on the ideas, suggestions and tactics I provide in this book. Some of the greatest emails I receive are from bar students who take the time out to share with me that they just passed their bar exam and want me to know how some of the specific information I shared with them helped.

This is especially memorable because I have been on the same journey they were on. I have been on the same journey you are on – the journey of the bar exam taker.

You read my circumstances going into my bar exam. There were plenty of reasons why I should not have passed the bar exam. But there was one stronger reason why I felt I should pass. The following belief:

"If others have passed the bar exam, so can I."

This attitude would be the seed I nurtured and grew during my prep.

I wish I knew what I am about to share with you before I took my bar exam. It calls to mind that wonderful quote, "If I only knew then, what I know now."

I have put the information into a step-by-step, systemized regimen that you can follow to bar exam success. I encourage you try on anything I suggest here and see how it fits for you. If it does, take it and move with it. If not, leave it and do it your way.

Remember that this is <u>your</u> bar exam. You know yourself better than I do or than any bar prep program does. Stick with study habits that you are comfortable using. But, allow me to be your guide on your bar exam journey.

To your success on your journey as a bar exam passer.

Dustin

Table of Contents

*see details at the end of the book

The 7 Steps to Bar Exam Success

STEP ONE
The 12 Key Concepts to Know for Bar Exam Success

To be successful and confident on your bar exam, here are the 12 Keys you should know.

Key #1: Have the Right K. A. B. – Knowledge, Actions, and Beliefs

In a broad sense, the bar exam really comes down to these three components:

1. Right Knowledge

Having the right knowledge means knowing *what to study.* You don't need to know all the rules, and you do not need to study all the bar exam materials you get. The key is knowing what is most important to study.

Usually, this means knowing what is typically tested on the exam. The bar examiners like to rinse and repeat questions constantly. If you get in-sync with what they typically test on each issue, then you will be saving time and energy.

For example, according to Bar/Bri in 2010, about 75% of the Evidence portion of the MBE will cover

Hearsay, Character, and Impeachment questions. Thus, if you get these three areas down, you will pass the Evidence MBE.

So, why are you studying anything else? Get those areas down cold and you pass. The other 25% will be so scattered about, studying for all of it will be like finding a needle in a haystack. Focus on the important stuff that is tested often.

Not all rules are created equal. If you give equal time to memorizing each rule, you are assuming each rule has the same chance of coming up on the bar exam, which is not true. Some issues and rules come up very frequently, while some come up once in a blue moon. It is very important you focus on the needle-movers.

Another example is the section on contracts essays. At least in California, they are very likely to test you on Latches because it always seems to show up in Contracts essays questions. These similar rules apply for all the topics. Figure out the important stuff and spend most of your time studying that material, not everything under the sun.

2. Right Actions

The second step is to take the right action. This is so important. You can waste a lot of time taking actions that do nothing for you. Do not be the hamster, who runs around in circles and at the end of the day does not move any closer towards your goal.

The 7 Steps to Bar Exam Success

The best action you can take is doing practice exams, over and over. Do not waste your time reviewing class lecture notes or reading rules over and over in a fatal attempt at rote memorization.

Instead, do practice tests and learn how the rules work within the context of the questions. After all, that is what you will be tested on come bar exam day, is it not? Why are you doing anything else?

Do you think football champions prepare by reading playbooks all week? No, they go out there and practice the actual plays under actual performance conditions, as best they can. That is how the pros do it. You are a pro too- so get out there and practice.

3. Right Beliefs

In the end, it all comes down to your beliefs. You can spend hours, weeks, and years taking bar exams and doing all the right things, but if you do not believe you can pass, it will all be for naught.

We all deal with self-doubt and belief issues during the bar exam. In fact, a little doubt is healthy because it is a fierce motivator. Think of the boy in the movie Life of Pi, when he was living in a small life boat lost at sea with a tiger, named Richard Parker, who was trying to eat him. Richard Parker represented the boy's fear, and the boy was grateful for the tiger because it kept the boy sharp. The fear kept the boy alive.

A little fear is good, but a lot is not. Use some of the techniques I give in Step 2 to conquer your fear. Also, be sure to get the sleep relaxation mp3 for free by visiting http://IPassedMyBarExam.com/TheSevenSteps.

Key #2: Become a Minimally Competent D Student

I know it's rough to think that way. After all, you did not make it to or through law school by getting D's on your final exams. Well, guess what? D's are the new A's!

You are probably going to beat yourself up a lot if you don't understand and implement this mindset. If you miss almost half the points on a practice MBE, do not freak out. Even, if you miss 80 out of 200 questions, you are probably still beyond passing.

If you get a 65 percent, you become a lawyer. 65! Can you believe it? That certainly would get you grounded by your parents in elementary school. And now, it will get you certified to have the fate of other's lives in your hands.

In practicality, the key is to know you do not have to get all the information in. You do not need to know all the rules, all the law, do all the homework, practice all the essays, or understand how everything works. You only need to know 65% of what you will be tested on. Usually if you focus on the needle-movers, as I stated above and get those down well, you will be A- ok! (or should I say D-ok?)

Key #3: Enjoy Peeling Onions

You have a lot of material to get through and even if you have seen it before, it will take a few run-throughs to really get it all down. That means you will probably have to look at the materials multiple times, re-take the same essays, re-do MBE questions, and re-read rules in order to get all this stuff down.

It is just how your mind works. Know that with every run-through of the material you are peeling off another layer of the onion and moving one step closer towards the beautiful onion core. Just try not to cry along the way!

Key #4: Know the Purpose of the Bar Exam

There is only one purpose of the bar exam. The purpose of the bar exam is to test your ability to pass the bar exam.

People get away from this too easily. The bar exam is not designed to test your ability as a lawyer or to see if you were good enough to graduate from law school. After all, name one lawyer you know that has 5,000 rules memorized? None! The bar examiners know you will look up the law once you get into that law office. It is also not a secondary test to see if you should have made it through law school.

The test is just like all other tests. It is a test to see if you can, well, pass the test. It is not a measure of how good of an attorney you will be. So, just focus on passing the test. Do whatever the grader wants you to do and do it well. Don't get cute, creative, or fancy. Be bland and methodical, like a dry martini, and you will be fine. Martinis pass the bar. Margaritas do not.

Key #5: Practice. Practice. Practice.

The number one reason people don't pass is because (see above, I wrote it three times). It is the bar exam version of buying a house. Instead of location, location, location, it is all in the practice.

However, do not just B.S. your practice. Make sure you are taking timed tests, especially for the essays and performance tests. Seriously. This was told to me by several people, and you will not find a single person who passed that does not emphasize the importance of this. It is the number one reason I passed. I took lots of practice tests and reviewed my answers in comparison to sample answers. Then, I went back and retook the tests to see if I could make mine closer to the sample answer.

When comparing your answer with the sample answer, ask yourself, did I use the same rules? Did I word the rules correctly? Did I spot all the issues?

Did I use all the facts? Go through a couple times until you get those essays down cold. That, my friends, is the key.

Key #6: Manage Your Energy, Not Just Your Time

I know, time management is cool, but sometimes you just cannot study, right? You just hit that wall? If you are like me, you will need breaks, exercise, a healthy eating plan, fresh air, social connection, and a good walk in nature every week.

Find that careful balance between focus and procrastination; between persistence and lack of commitment. It is a careful balance. Sometimes you just need a break, and sometimes you are just being lazy.

What is the point in spending eight hours studying if you are too brain-fried to retain anything? Instead, if you spent two hours exercising, showering, and eating a good meal, you could spend the next six hours very effectively. Six hours of fresh energy is better than eight hours of stagnant energy.

Here is a test to see if you are just procrastinating or really need to manage your energy. If you are trying to study and just cannot do it, check off the following:

- Did I exercise in the last three days?
- Did I eat a good meal in the last four hours or snack in the last hour (Starbucks and donuts do not count)?
- Have I been outside in the sun for at least 30 minutes consistently in the last two days?
- Have I had a glass of water in the last two hours?

If you do not pass the above tests, then get on it. If you do pass the tests, then just try studying for at least 15 to 30 minutes. If you still cannot do it and feel like you are hitting a brick wall, then you need a mental break. Take a few hours off and go do something fun like watching a movie or getting a massage.

And do not make yourself feel guilty for taking a break by wondering, "What will everyone else think of me if they find out I'm watching a movie and 'should' be studying?" They will think you are awesome and congratulate you for being in charge of your own energy and life! They will also congratulate you for preventing burn out and passing the bar.

Hey, I took four days off only three weeks out from my bar to get ready for the final push. I took singing and acting classes during my bar prep. And you know what, the classes helped me very much!

So, take your break, then come back and study. The bottom line is, you must manage your energy. The bar exam is a marathon, not a sprint. If you force yourself through studying too hard, especially early on, you will burn out. Pace yourself.

Slow and steady wins the race. Re-charge along the way. A car will not make it to its destination across the country if it were not for gas stations along the way. You have time, plenty of time to be prepared enough. Don't force your way through.

Key #7: Be a Sheep

I am sure you have heard this already. On your tests, blend in with the crowd. Don't get creative or cute. Be boring, direct, and dry. If the graders actually remember or notice your essay in the midst of all the other essays, that is not a good thing. Do what the crowd is doing, don't stand out, and you will be fine.

Key #8: Work Hard and Smart

There is no getting around it. The bar exam is about doing the hard work. It is about persistence and moving forward in the face of adversity, doubt, and fear.

But, it is also about working smart. Do not be a hamster on a hamster wheel that burns all his energy, but at the end of the day ends up right back where he started. Work smart by following the keys outlined in this book, such as practicing exams and studying the needle-moving content.

Your success is all determined in your preparation. There is no 'getting lucky' on the bar exam. There is no conspiracy to pass only a certain amount of people. You and you alone have the power and responsibility for your success. Prepare well and follow the tips outlined in this book and you should be well on your way to success on your bar exam.

Key #9: Run Away from Pessimists

I mean it. Run. If you see someone walking your way bawking their head off about how horrible their life is and the bar exam is, grab your book bags and head for the hills.

Misery loves company and negative pessimists love to get rid of their negative energy by spilling it onto you. And every bar class has a few of these. Guess what? They are scared they will not be passing the bar exam, and want you to be scared with them!

You do not need to hang out with them, and you should just avoid them. Keep positive. Yes, you can do this. We all have doubt, but spewing it out into the atmosphere in front of all others to see is not a healthy way of going about it.

Instead, handle negative emotions appropriately by journaling them away or speaking about them to a friend, relative, or professional therapist (professional therapy is awesome, do not get all taboo on me!).

Key #10: The Graders Want You to Pass

Yes, I said it. Read it again. They like you and want you to pass! They pass more people every year than they fail, so that must mean something, right? They are normal human beings who have been through what you have been through (that is if we can we call lawyers 'normal'). They can empathize. Just do your work, prepare well and give it your best.

Key #11: Be Grateful You Get to Take the Bar Exam

Do you know how many people in this world would love to be in your shoes? 1% of the world gets to attend college, let alone law school. You are taking the entrance exam to become a part of the most elite profession in the most elite country in the history of planet Earth!

There will be many challenges and plenty of opportunities to complain during the bar exam, but you can at least be grateful you have had the opportunity and choice to be where you are at. You can be grateful for your health, success, and happiness up to this point.

Getting into a state of gratitude not only places you more into reality, it will also ground you and attract more success and circumstances to be grateful for, like passing bar results!

Key #12: You Can Do It

Do not overhype this stupid bar exam. It is not this crazy Mt. Everest thing that everyone likes to make a big deal out of. Just do what needs to be done. Practice your stuff and do the work. Be cool when you walk into the exam room. You have made it through law school for goodness sake. Don't you remember 1st year when you wanted to tear the sheets out of your book one by one, and shred them into little itty bitty pieces, then watch them slowly burn in a flame? (Was that just me?)

This test is so within your capabilities. Did you read my story in the introduction? I graduated in the bottom half of my class, barely passed my writing classes, failed the MPRE (twice actually), and still passed the bar in California. Boooya! If this guy can do it, you are on your way.

Be sharp. Be diligent. Prepare well. Do your best. And you will crush it.

STEP TWO
The Bar Exam Passer's Mind and Body

The Mind

Mindset is key. You will not find a single personal development book or super successful person that does not emphasize the importance of mindset above anything else.

I do not want to go too much into mindset theory here. After all, you do have a bar exam to study for. Instead, I will give you some practical techniques to supercharge your mind. I actually have an entire separate program to amplify your bar exam mind, but I'll give you some of my really good stuff here.

Empowering Mind Technique #1 – Know thy Purpose

The first question you should really ask during your bar exam is the following:

"Why do I want to pass the bar exam?"

If you have a strong enough WHY, you will be able to surmount the challenges and obstacles along the way. And the more you make your WHY about how you will benefit others, the more powerful it will be.

For me, I didn't even want to practice law, so I definitely had a hard time with this question. Here's what I thought of when I did this exercise:

- Be complete with the law school experience
- Have the certification just in case I decide to practice law
- I'll try it once and go for it full force, but if I don't pass I won't take it again

These reasons are ok, but at the end of the day they didn't really motivate me for success. The big motivator was this one:

Bar exam results came out Friday, May 14th. Bar exam graduation ceremony was Saturday, May 15th. My brother's birthday was also Saturday, May 15th. I thought ahead and knew it be awesome for my mom, who has helped me so much through law school, to celebrate my graduation, my brother's birthday, and passing bar results all in the same weekend! But, wouldn't it be just bittersweet if I did not pass the bar?

Believe it or not, that was my huge motivation. Notice it had nothing to do with being an attorney. It was a reason that was outside of myself. I was thinking of others and how it would be special for my mom.

It is sort of a silly reason to want to pass the bar exam, but it works. So, get a journal, and take some time right now and write out your answer to the question. "Why do you want to pass the bar exam?" And make sure you include reasons of how others will benefit.

Empowering Mind Technique #2 – Flip the Switch of Negative Self-Talk

Flip the negative self-talk switch. Many people get anxiety because they are focusing on the wrong question. They may ask themselves, "What if I do not pass the bar exam?" Then, their brain will go into a whole host of fearful, negative scenarios that will happen.

If you are experiencing this, just flip the question. Ask yourself, "What if I *do* pass the bar exam?" Then, your mind will start thinking about all the wonderful things that will happen for you. The more you ask yourself positive, empowering questions, the more you allow your mind to explore the possibilities, generate the feelings of success, and align you with passing the bar exam.

Here are a few more questions to ask yourself:
- What if I pass the essays?
- What if I pass the MBE?
- Why am I doing so well and being so calm during the bar process?
- Why am I able to figure out this question right now?

The more empowering questions you ask throughout the bar prep, the more your mind will focus on those positive outcomes and determine how they can be created in your life. Whenever you feel the stress, ask a positive question.

Empowering Mind Technique #3 – The Power Affirmations

Affirmations are simply positive statements you consciously tell yourself to re-program your mind. Believe it or not, you don't actually believe the truth. You only believe what you have been exposed to over the years from the words, actions, and body language of your parents, peer group, and society.

Some people believe their fears and falsities more than they do the truth. The truth is that <u>anyone</u> can pass the bar exam. So this technique is about using positive statements to align yourself with your best self.

The following is a list of affirmations. If you can print them out and put them by your bed or on your bathroom mirror that would be best. Read this, out loud, three times every single day during your bar exam prep. You can do it in the once in the morning, once in the afternoon, and once in the evening or read it all at once. I don't want to get too much into the science of it, but it works and works very well. So, do it. In fact, I will send you copy of this page so you can print it out and post it on your wall if you go to http://IPassedMyBarExam.com/TheSevenSteps.

I can pass the bar exam

I am worthy, confident, and capable

People like and enjoy seeing me succeed and be happy

The bar exam is easy, fun, and doable

I like and enjoy studying for the bar exam

Why am I doing so well on all my practice tests?

Why am I becoming more and more confident each and every day?

I am bar exam passer

Others have done it, so can I

I believe in myself fully and completely

I cannot wait to see my passing results

It is [insert date results are released here], and I just received news that I passed my bar exam. I am so excited!

I am a confident and calm test taker

I am a practicing attorney right now

"Congratulations counselor!"

My name appears on the pass list

I can't wait to share my passing results with friends and family

I am prepared, diligent, and I work hard and smart

I am unstoppable

If you read those affirmations every day, you are going to be so far ahead of the game, it is not even funny. By the way, I have a 20 minute audio version of similar affirmations and much more, very Louise Hay-style, designed specifically for the bar exam. You can get it by going to http://IPassedMyBarExam.com/Affirmations.

Empowering Mind Technique #4 – The Bar Exam Passer's Script

This is another great technique. Same rules as above apply, in that you should print it out and read it out loud. This is more involved, and you don't have to read it as much to get the same effect. Read it anywhere from twice to four times per week.

The script is on the next page, and I will send you a copy you can print out too. Just go to http://IPassedMyBarExam.com/TheSevenSteps.

It is now [insert date of results], and I [insert name], found out I passed my bar exam. I did a great job taking and passing my bar exam. I was disciplined and diligent in my studying, taking breaks as needed. I did a very good job learning the law and memorizing the relevant rules I needed to pass my bar exam. I did a good job supporting, encouraging, and giving positive energy and support to others.

I enjoyed my bar exam prep study. I did a good job taking practice essays and getting myself ready. I was confident and focused, and prepared as a bar exam passer would prepare. I was very good at issue spotting and giving good analysis in a concise manner as the bar exam grader wants me to. I did a very good job remembering the rules and applying them to the fact pattern in a manner that made me pass the bar exam.

Even if there were things I didn't know, I did a good job making up rules on the go, applying the facts, and giving good analysis such that I passed my bar exam.

I was able to learn with ease and confidence. I did a very good job preparing for my MBE test, learning and applying the law to the questions and getting the right answers, enough to pass the bar exam.

I stayed strong and sturdy throughout my bar exam prep. The bar exam graders and people wanted me to pass. They encouraged and supported me. The bar exam graders enjoyed reading my essay and giving me passing scores.

I did a very good job on my performance test. I learned how to take them very well and did take them very well on my bar exam.

I felt good, excited, and proud when I finished my bar exam. I just knew I did very well and passed.

On bar exam results day, I checked my results and saw that I passed the bar exam!!! I was so excited and happy! I shared with my family, friends, and relatives. Everyone was so proud of me, and I was proud of myself.

Now it is time to go to the next phase of my life. I was very grateful I had the opportunity to take and pass the bar exam.

I passed my bar exam naturally, readily, and easily.

For these techniques to be effective, it is all about consistency and repetition. If you can add some emotion of excitement and belief in there and read it as if it's already true, then you'll be tripling the positive effects of it. If you are consistent with the readings, you are supercharging your mind to success.

If you like these techniques, check out the awesome program I have that will really supercharge your mind, called the Bar Exam Mental Edge: http://IPassedMyBarExam.com/BarExamMentalEdge

The Body

If the mind is the most important part of the bar exam, then the body is the most overlooked part of the bar exam. Many people think their stress, feelings of overwhelm, lack of sleep, and headaches during the bar exam come from the stress of studying the material.

Although, that is partially true, much of it is also probably caused by the fact that they are not managing their body and energy. If you want to hear some of the philosophy on this, I did a podcast on the bar exam body. You can listen to it and my other podcasts at http://IPassedMyBarExam.com/Podcasts.

I once had a bar exam client come to me to help her reduce anxiety through the use of visualization and relaxation techniques. During our conversations, I found out at what times of the day she was feeling anxiety. I then asked about her eating habits. She drank coffee in the morning with a piece of toast and had a muffin for lunch.

No wonder she had anxiety! The body is like a gas tank. It needs fuel to run. If you don't fuel your body with proper food frequently, it will automatically think there is something wrong and go into starvation mode. When it does, it sends small doses of adrenaline to your muscles and puts you in a hyper-aware state so you can stop what you are doing, get up, and go find food to survive.

Do you think you can sit, study, and output extraordinary amounts of mental energy preparing for the bar exam when your body is tensing up and telling you to go get food?

Absolutely not.

It goes back to Key #6. Manage your energy.

As for the coffee, did you know coffee actually increases the cortisol in your body? Do you know what cortisol does? Cortisol is the stress hormone in your body and when it goes up, so does your stress. Literally, coffee stresses you out.

I'm not saying to drop the coffee, especially if you're semi-addicted. But, if you're feeling stressed, do not blame the bar exam. Blame what you are putting into your body.

That being said, here are 11 Bar Exam body techniques to supercharge your body and energy to efficient studying and bar exam success.

1. Drink 100 ounces of water per day

I will admit that I usually underestimate the importance of water and do not think I really feel the benefits. But, when I pay attention to the difference in my mind and body when I do drink water and when I don't, I start being very proactive in this area.

Quick Tip
Did you know the number one cause of headaches in America is de-hydration? Drink up!

The government recommends the average American drink 64 ounces of water per day. Well, the average American also watches television four hours per day. Right now, you are not the average American. You are a bar exam student and expending lots of mental energy. If you are outputting lots of energy, you should be inputting lots of energy. Water clears your body of toxins and cleans up your system so you are feeling good and thinking straight.

So, drink 100 ounces. That is about 3 liters, or 1.5 bottles of Sprite. Of course, fill it with water, not Sprite. Drink a 16 ounce glass about every hour you are studying and you will be doing great.

2. Get 30 minutes of outdoor air and sunlight every day

Your body is not built to remain inside an underground library for too long. It needs its vitamin D and fresh energy. If you're getting a headache or feel like your energy is stagnant, take a brisk walk outside for 30 minutes.

It is a great way to clear your head, allow the information to process in your brain, and get your natural energy all at the same time. If you can get into nature, it is even better. Although walking a city is better than nothing, going on a walk in a park, the mountains, or by a lake, ocean, or the river will be best.

3. Take a 5 minute break every 60-90 minutes

The latest studies in High Performance and neuroscience demonstrate that people who take about a five-minute break every hour or so will report higher levels of energy and be 25% more productive. So take more breaks, and you increase your productivity and energy!

What you do on those breaks is important. It should not just be a Facebook check. To get the 25% boost, you must 1) Disengage from your current work, and 2) Move your body around.

Disengagement simply means doing something else. Let your mind take a break from the studying and do something else for a few minutes. Moving the body around would be a simple walk to the bathroom, grabbing a glass of water, or taking a quick lap around the house. Do these and you'll have higher energy and more productivity!

4. Exercise 3 times per week

This is very important. Get at least 20 minutes of cardio three times per week. To be a high performer, make one of those cardio at least an hour – long, like a Zumba or bicycle class. You do not need to be going at full speed. An hour at half-speed does the trick.

Thousands of studies have shown that exercise releases tension and makes you sharper and more focused. It relieves stress and releases endorphins, which are your body's natural happy drug. Schedule your exercise routine. If you can even make one of the routines a fun sport you like to play, that will be even better because you are having more fun and strengthening your creativity skills, which is needed for sanity during the bar exam.

5. Sleep 7 to 9 hours per night

Sleeping less is not the cool way to go. In fact, if you go three days of less than six hours per sleep in a row, your cognitive scores begin to drop at a rate of 15% per day! Do it for five days and you will have lost ½ of your cognitive ability. Then, it takes another 4 to 6 days of full 7 hour rest to get back up to 90%. So, like your momma said when you were growing up – get to bed!

Having trouble sleeping? Be sure to download my bar exam sleeping mp3. It is free. Just go to http://IPassedMyBarexam.com/TheSevenSteps and play it while you go to sleep.

If you listen to it and still can't sleep, make sure you didn't drink any coffee or caffeinated tea before sleeping. If it's still a problem, then do the following, which worked for me:

A) Tell yourself how tired you are and start yawning

Start pretending to be tired. Fake yawn, and tell yourself how sleepy you are. Your body will start to follow.

B) Meditate before you sleep

Go find a nice peaceful place in your home, put on the "White noise" playlist in Pandora.com, close your eyes, and just focus on your breath. Do this for 20 minutes and you'll probably have a hard time staying up.

C) Read a book before you sleep

Have you ever tried to read at night, but it just put you to bed? Now is the time to do it! Read a novel or try reading a long list of bar exam rules, like the mini-conviser book from Bar/Bri, and you will be asleep in no time.

D) Read your affirmations

If you cannot sleep, your spirit could be telling you to program some positivity into your mind before sleep. That is your affirmations. Affirmations are best read at night because your mind spends the next eight hours processing them into your subconscious. To get your bar exam affirmations from this book, go to http://IPassedMyBarExam.com/TheSevenSteps.

6. Cut back on the sugar and caffeine

Happy food is cool, but excess is not. I already said it above, but excess sugar, coffee, and caffeine increase your stress levels. Water is a great alternative.

7. Know your body clock

Some people are morning peeps. Some are night owls. Morning peeps might be ready to go right off the bat. Or they might be excited to start with a morning jog, shower, good breakfast or exercise and get to it. Morning peeps have their best study time first thing in the morning and start to drop off in mid-afternoon, where doing lighter studying or running errands can be better.   Do practice tests in the morning and note reviewing in the afternoon.

Night owls want to start slow and warm up. Running errands or doing lighter studying in the morning would be better, with the important and heavier studying coming in late afternoon or evening. Do reviewing and memorizing in the morning and practice exams later on.

8. Break Ideas

When you are taking some time off, considering doing these activities to get the most out of replenishing your mind and body. If you want to take a short break, here are some ideas:

- Walk your dog
- Read your favorite book
- Play video games
- Watch YouTube videos
- Do a quick round of push-ups
- Call family or a friend
- Take a power nap
- Eat a snack
- Sing to yourself

For those of you wanting to take a several hour or day-long break, here are some ideas:

- Go to the gym
- Swim
- Get a massage
- Go on a date
- See a movie
- Ski or snowboard
- Go to the beach
- Take a bubble bath
- Go out to a bar or night club
- Go to church
- Drive around the city
- Get a haircut or a manicure
- Go to a concert
- Play or watch sports

9. Meditate and Visualize

Did you know they are currently teaching elementary school children the scientific benefits of meditation? Where was that when I was a kid?! Meditation is a proven technique for stress and anxiety relief. Even some hospitals will tell you to try meditation before giving you anti-anxiety pills.

If you can add some creative visualization, while you are meditating, then you are practicing the techniques that Oprah, Anthony Hopkins, and Olympic athletes credit for their success. Every night, spend twenty minutes meditating and visualizing yourself passing the bar exam. See yourself opening the results page and seeing your name on the pass list. Visualize a great bar exam week. Visualize how you and your family and friends will celebrate.

Entire libraries have been written on the meditation and visualization process. I have spent 750 hours and one entire year training on how to help people better visualize their results. Get your very own visualization and meditation mp3 package that I designed specifically for passing the bar exam at http://IPassedMyBarExam.com/BarExamMentalEdge. It also includes a vision board and an additional affirmation mp3.

10. Stretching and/or yoga

Yoga is awesome. It is like meditation and stretching combined into one. When you are sitting for hours every day, your body and energy become stagnant. By stretching the muscles out, you open your energy channels for flow again. Even if you do not want to do yoga, at least spend a few minutes daily stretching your hamstrings, quadriceps, and arms. It will release tension, increase blood circulation, and bring you more stamina and energy.

11. Eat 3 to 4 meals per day. Have a snack every 2 hours.

We talked about eating. Now, let's talk about eating healthy. You want to put fuel in your tank, but it can't be just any fuel. Muffins and slices of bread will not get it done. I am not a doctor, and you should always consult your doctor when making changes to your diet (my legal disclaimer), but here are a few I recommend:

Larger meals:
- Fish – proven to increase brain strength and make you smarter
- Chicken – high on protein
- Veggies – plenty of greens, bell peppers, cucumbers, onions, tomatoes

Snacks:
- Green oat bars
- Almonds
- Carrots
- Bananas, apples, berries

Supplements

These supplements were recommended to me by the high performance guy Brendon Burchard. They are as organic and natural as can be. I have to say, since I started using them, my energy and productivity have gone up big-time! I mix these into my water bottle and drink throughout the day. It does wonders. Here is what I currently use, and they can be found on Amazon.com.

- Vega Protein
- Vega One
- Amazing Grass Green Superfood

Multi-vitamins
I use the Rainbow Organic brand.
- Multivitamin
- Calcium
- Omega-3

Put these mind and body tips into play and you will be feeling more energized and confident in no time!

Do you want more Mind and Body tips? Check out Lauren Fire's course on Bar Exam Anxiety and Mindset at
http://IPassedMyBarExam.com/MindOverBar.

STEP THREE
The 8 Questions to ask Yourself Before you Begin Bar Prep

There are a few things to take care of before your bar exam prep even begins. You may be reading this after you have begun bar prep. If that is the case, just take what applies and leave the rest.

1. What bar prep program should you take, if any?

Those who take bar prep programs have a higher pass rate than those who do not. That statement is backed by factual data. That should make sense. If someone is going to be paying money for a bar prep program, they had better do better than those going at it alone. The real question is, should *you* take a bar prep program?

Bar Prep Company vs. Prepare on Your Own

Here are some criteria to consider:

A) Cost

Bar prep programs can cost a lot of money, but failing the bar exam also costs a lot of money. There are six to eight months of wasted time and lost potential income you could have had if you were working. If you get a job after you find out you passed at a salary of $50,000, you are looking at $25,000 to $35,000 in lost potential income, based on the fact that you took an extra half-year to study!

Then, there is the fact that the interest on your loan is accruing. There are also costs for the time and headache of having to retake the bar exam. So, yes, bar prep programs can cost a lot of money, but sometimes it is worth the payment.

B) Your jurisdiction

If you are in a jurisdiction like California, where the summer pass rate is typically around 53% and the winter is less than 40%, you may want to get on the bar prep bandwagon. If you are in a jurisdiction where the pass rate is high, then self study may be ok. Also, look at what is available. Some bar prep companies are not available in all jurisdictions.

C) ABA vs. non-ABA school?

I don't want to say it, but the statistics speak for themselves. Non-ABA law schools have a drastically lower bar pass rate than ABA-accredited schools. For the July 2012 bar exam, California ABA students had a 76.9% pass rate. Out of state ABA students had a 63.6%. The non-ABA pass rate was less than 33%. If you went to an ABA-approved school, your training is better. For non-ABA, you definitely want to go with a bar prep program, especially one that helps with the writing.

D) How well did you do in law school?

If you were a super star student in a high pass jurisdiction, then maybe you don't need a bar prep program. But, in my ABA-approved school, there was a girl in the class ahead of me who finished in the top 10 of her class. She took the bar without a bar prep program and guess what... she failed. The bar exam is different from law school exams. You are best served with a specific system and program.

E) 1st time taker, Repeater, or Foreign Attorney

I hate to bring this up too because I fundamentally believe anyone can pass the bar exam. I don't mention these stats to discourage you, but rather to help you be aware of reality so you can best prepare. The reason California bar exam pass rates are so low is largely due to repeaters.

In the July 2012 California bar exam, nearly one in every four takers was a repeater. 1st time takers had a 68.3% pass rate. Repeaters were 18.1%, dropping the state pass rate to 55.3%. Foreign attorneys were well under 20%.

If you fall into these stats, then get a professional coach/tutor/program to help you out. Many good students in ABA-approved schools are even taking bar prep programs. Personally, I think everyone should take a bar prep program.

The bar exam is such a specific test, it's important to hire a professional, who studies the intricacies of the test for a living. It will likely save you lots of time, money, and headache down the road.

I know these can be discouraging statistics and again, my goal is not to discourage you. In fact, I hope you get so mad at me for bringing this up you decide to prove you are going to pass and tell this statistic to shove it! Remember, <u>anyone</u> can pass the bar exam with the right preparation! Go get it!

Myth-Buster
"If I am a repeater, I have a significantly less chance of passing the bar exam."
That is not true. Although, statistically repeaters have a lower pass rate, your bar exam is still completely in your hands! There is no reason why you have any less chance than anyone else. But, if you are repeating, you need to find your mistakes to learn and improve from the past. If you just repeat the same study method, you risk getting the same results. Learn and improve.

Which bar prep company to take?

Now, that I have convinced you to take a bar prep company, the next question is, which one? Here are a few I would recommend:

A) Bar/Bri

You knew this was coming. Bar/Bri is the oldest and most established program, and it seems everyone takes it. I recommend it because I used it, it was good, and I passed. Thousands of people pass with Bar/Bri every single year.

But, there are a few problems with Bar/Bri.
- It is super expensive (nearly $4,000)
- It does not publish pass rates
- You are one of thousands and there is little personalized attention

B) Themis

Due to the problems stated above, a group of former Bar/Bri employees decided to jump ship and form their own company around 2009 called Themis Bar Prep. They are completely online-based and offer a competitive price point of about $1,500 for their program.

They also boast very nice pass rates and actually publish them. They claim to have pass rates of 74% in California and 90% in New York! But, these pass rates are only amongst 1st time takers, who completed at least 75% of their assignments. The pass rate amongst all 1st time takers in California is 68.3%, so arguably Themis is doing only a little better than average.

The only other problem with Themis also may be an advantage. They do not have in-class lectures. Everything is at the hands of your computer. You can order actual materials as well, but if you need a classroom environment and a peer group to keep you accountable, you won't find that with Themis, but you will at Bar/Bri.

Nonetheless, I have searched far and beyond amongst the forums and significantly more often than not, I see positive reviews. I also had several friends use Themis, and I give it my thumbs up.

C) BarMax

Then there is BarMax. BarMax was founded in 2010, by a former Harvard law graduate. It is completely mobile-based. You run everything from either your Iphone, Ipod, or Ipad. BarMax could be the wave of the future, as the former President and founder of Bar/Bri recently left and joined BarMax!

I had the opportunity to test a trial version of BarMax on my Ipod touch, and it is both a great program and very easy to use. It also has good reviews in the Itunes store, and it was created by the same company which provides LSAT max, which has awesome reviews on Amazon.

BarMax also does not have an in-class environment, but it is cooler than Themis because you can literally study anywhere you have your Ipod. The program is loaded onto your app, so unlike Themis or Bar/Bri, no internet connection is required, meaning no lag or down-time (which many students have complained about with Themis.)

If you want to study outdoors or go on a jog while listening to lectures, BarMax is your program. If you don't have an Apple device, they have options where they will give you one at a discounted price if you get their program.

It gets even cooler because the pass rate for BarMax is almost the same as Themis. BarMax 2012 was 73% for California and 83% for New York (up from their 2011 pass rates of 71% and 81% respectively), and that pass rate is amongst all people who used BarMax, not just 1st time takers completing a certain amount of assignments. It is even more impressive considering that many BarMax users are repeat takers. If a program can boast that good of a pass rate, they must be doing something right?

BarMax also happens to be the least expensive of the bar prep programs mentioned. You can get it in the Apple store for a low price of $999. That is significant. All those who thought bar prep programs like Bar/Bri were too expensive now have a good, viable option with BarMax.

By the way, I worked out an exclusive deal with BarMax for readers of this book. If you purchase BarMax through this link http://IPassedMyBarExam.com/BarMax, you can actually save an additional $150 on the program! Wowzer! In addition, if you decide to go with their Ipad version, you can almost get the Ipad for free with the discount!

D) Celebration Bar Review

I do not have any personal experience with them, nor do I know anyone who took them, but I do know their founder Jackson Mumey, who has been doing bar prep for 20 years and boasts an overall 80% pass rate in California.

I have found some reviews of this program from students who were absolutely in love with the Celebration Bar style of prep. They have even volunteered their email address so you can email them and ask questions about the program. I had the pleasure of interviewing Jackson and you can listen to him at http://IPassedMyBarExam.com/Podcasts.

E) Kaplan

Plain and simply, I do not recommend you go with Kaplan. Their all-in-one program is still new to the bar scene, they do not publish their pass rate, and I have seen terrible reviews of them online. Also, their price point is only slightly under Bar/Bri. If you are going to fork over that much money, you might as well go with Bar/Bri.

Myth-Buster
"If I take a bar prep program, it will give me everything I need to prepare."
While that is largely true, most bar prep programs are missing a key component, which is improving your writing ability. They presume you know how to write in a 'lawyerly' style already. Many people do all the

right things, but do not have a 'lawyerly' writing style, so they fail. Improve your writing by re-writing good sample answers or hiring a tutor.

Still not convinced about taking a bar prep program?

If you are still not convinced about taking a bar prep program, then you want to make sure you are at least getting the right materials to study for. Here are a few that I recommend.

Jessica Klein's Be a Goat Book

Jessica is the author of the Be a Goat bar exam blog. Not only is she the nicest lady you will ever meet, she has shared her bar exam experiences in her latest book <u>Be A Goat</u>. Jessica is a self-studier and a bar exam repeater. She was one of the few in California to pass the bar after failing it a first time and never using a bar prep program. She provides a step-by-step guide to passing the bar in her book, including time tables and what resources she used. Her book is rated all 5 stars on Amazon as of this writing! You can save $15 on her book by going to http://IPassedMyBarExam.com/BeAGoat and entering the code: 94ZVXNQJ

BarEssays

I told you how important it is to practice essays. One of the issues is reviewing practice answers. You can look at the state bar model answers, which I do not recommend because those answers are much better than what you need to pass. Another option is to use the Bar/Bri essay guide book. This is a better option, but you are still comparing your answers to a doctored response, not an actual answer.

Then came BarEssays.com. The founder, Gil Peles from UC Berkeley law school, spent years compiling a database of actual, graded bar exams. He created a searchable database, where you can view actual answers to any California essay and performance test question since 2004. You can also view actual bar grader notes on some of the answers.

By doing this, you can compare your practice essays to other graded essays to see how well you would fare. You can see what a score of an 80 looks like, a 60, or even a 40 for the essays. You can even view some handwritten essays. Also, his website is really easy to use. You can search by Year, Topic, or scores received.

I worked out a deal with Gil also. Sign up for his site at http://IPassedMyBarExam.com/BarEssays, and I will give you a free copy of one of my bar exam products. You can also save $15 on his program. He doesn't want the discount code going viral, so just go to http://IPassedMyBarExam.com/Bed or send me an email (Dustin@IPassedMyBarExam.com), and I'll hook you up with his $15-off discount code!

Adaptibar

If BarEssays will cover you on the essays, then Adaptibar will cover you on the MBE. Adaptibar is one of the go-to sources for MBE test prep. They use only licensed questions, so unlike some bar prep programs, all their prep questions are real. They also claim that your score on Adaptibar exams will be within 96% determinative of your score on the bar exam, so you know how you are doing before you head into the exam.

They also have many other options that allow you take simulated exams, focusing on specific subjects. You can also focus on specific topics within subjects, like only Battery for Torts questions. They have very good reviews online. You can save $50 and get a free copy of my affirmation mp3 if you sign up through this link! http://IPassedMyBarExam.com/Adaptibar.

2. **Work during the bar exam?**

To work or not to work, that is the question. I have heard many stories of people who worked and passed the bar exam. Just ask Jessica Zaylia who posted several YouTube videos describing her bar exam experience:
http://IPassedMyBarExam.com/Jessica

Some things to ask yourself:

- Will you be ok financially if you don't work?
- Can you pull money from savings or get a short-term loan?
- Can you take a temporarily leave of absence from work?
- How much time and energy can you devote to each of your work and bar exam studying commitments?
- How well do you manage yourself? For example, can you do 8-hour work days, then 4-hour study periods?
- Will you lose your job if you stop working?
- Do you want to keep your job after the bar exam anyway?
- What is the pass rate in your jurisdiction?
- What is the worst that would happen if you didn't work?
- What is the worst that would happen if you did work?
- Do you understand and learn the material more quickly and easily than most?

If you absolutely must work, try to work out an arrangement with your employer through any of the following:

- Take an extra day off per week
- Work 10 hour days for four days to get an extra day off

- Work part-time, either mornings or afternoon for two months
- Work from home
- Work on your own time
- Take the last three weeks off before the bar exam to study full time

If you can get away without working, doing so is probably better, although opinions will vary.

3. <u>What is your schedule outside of bar exam prep?</u>

Bar exam prep should definitely be your main focus during the bar exam. I will pass along a piece of advice I received that worked well for me:

"Whatever your life looked like before the bar exam should be the same during the bar exam."

Thus, don't make any significant changes to your lifestyle during the bar exam. Have it fit within whatever you were doing. If you were taking classes at a community college, continue taking them. If you were doing yoga, playing in a basketball intramural league, having Saturday night date night, etc., keep doing it. If you can, continue living where you were living before. If you were using study groups for law school finals, then continue doing so. If not, then don't start.

Also, it's important to schedule your other outside bar exam activities. The more you are able to schedule the actions, the more likely you are to actually do that action.

Schedule the following as best as you can:

- ***Exercise routines***

Find your favorite classes at your gym and get at it.

- ***Time off***

Many people like to spend one day per week where they do nothing bar exam related. What day would you do that?

- ***Fun activities***

It is important to do at least one fun activity per week. It should be completely non-bar related, preferably with people you enjoy, and that is really fun for you. It might be bowling, a movie, dinner, hiking, biking, swimming, playing Monopoly, favorite video game, family night, etc. The sustaining energy this activity provides is awesome.

4. <u>Who is in your support group?</u>

The bar exam will have its emotional upheavals, so it's good to have a list of people you can count on for some emotional support when the going gets tough.

Write out a list of three people you know you can count on to help you out during the tough times. Even hearing, "I know you can do it," can mean a world of difference. Of course, you can always email me at Dustin@IPassedMyBarExam.com for some motivation!

5. <u>Where will your post bar trip be?</u>

After the bar exam, it's time to celebrate! Where will you go? What will you do? Who will you be with? It is really important for you to schedule a fun reward for yourself. You have earned it.

Not only that, but studies have shown that if you have something to look forward to in the future, you will be more upbeat and excited in the present. If you are looking forward to a post-bar trip to Maui, won't you put more effort into your studies now? You will want to work harder to earn it.

When I was a kid, I was taking my black belt test, which included a very tough conditioning test on Saturday night. I told my mom I wanted her to make a bunch of chocolate chip cookies on Sunday, so I would have that to look forward to when I finished my test. And it worked! I kicked everyone's butt in the conditioning part of the test!

6. <u>Did you clear your workspace and house of clutter?</u>

Some of you are squeaky clean. Some of you are tornado-like messy. The bottom line is that if your car, house, and workspace environment are piled with books and papers, you are going to be more stressed out and overwhelmed.

Have you seen a lawyer's office that is just stacked with folders, papers, and books? Does it not stress you out just looking at it? Imagine if you had to work in that environment!

Well, some of you do, and it is going to make the road harder. I know now is not the time to try and change habits, but if you can give your workspace, room, house, and car a quick clean before you begin, you clear out your mind, creating a calmer bar exam experience.

7. <u>Do you have a book or CD to ground and inspire you?</u>

Some people like to see the higher purpose in what they are doing. I am all for it. If you have a spiritual book, like a bible, a book of poems, or inspiration near you that you can read at night, it can make all the difference in the world. Reading passages can help you through the rough times.

I know I am harping on this a lot, but I strongly suggest you get a copy of the Bar Exam Mental Edge as well. It has a complete set of visualization mp3's, bar exam affirmation audio set, a bar exam vision board, vision movie, and a whole host of other tools to ground, inspire, and set your mind on bar exam success. It is one of those programs I wish I had when taking the bar exam and some of the techniques are the very same I used for my bar exam! And depending on when you get it, there will likely be a no-risk bar exam pass money-back guarantee! You can get it at http://IPassedMyBarExam.com/BarExamMentalEdge.

8. <u>Do you have a music playlist?</u>

Science has shown that listening to certain types of music has proven benefits. Create your favorite playlist on your mp3 player or go to any of the following sites:

a) <u>Pandora.com</u>

You probably have heard about these guys. You just pick an artist and click play, then it will automatically create a playlist for you with similar music. You might hear an ad every hour, but everything is free. I'm listening to a Hans Zimmer soundtrack playlist as I write this!

b) Grooveshark.com

This is also a great site. You can pick amongst thousands of songs and create your own playlist. It is also free. Whereas, Pandora will pick the songs to play, if you have a specific song you want to play, just head on over to Grooveshark.

c) Relaxdaily.net

If you want to listen to wonderful, relaxing music, head on over to this site to download or stream free relaxing music that will help you study.

STEP FOUR
The 5 Most Frequently Asked Questions

We have finally reached the meat and bones of bar prep. How effectively you spend the next two months will dictate your success. The bar exam really is all about the preparation. Sometimes, I say 'good luck,' but I really think luck has very little to do with bar exam success. If luck is when preparation meets opportunity, well you can get lucky by preparing well because your opportunity is coming up in the next few weeks.

During the bar prep, I struggled big-time trying to figure out many things. In this chapter, I will go over the questions to which you probably have been begging for answers.

FAQ #1
When should I start studying for the bar Exam?

I struggled with this question during my winter break, prior to our bar prep start date. I wanted to get ahead, and I almost bought all twelve Emanuels Examples and Explanation topics for my bar exam because I was thinking, if I reviewed them over winter break, I would have a leg up during bar prep. Thankfully, I came to my senses first.

Here is the best answer to this question:

"Start studying when your bar prep program tells you to start studying"

People ask me all the time if they should start earlier than their bar prep program. I give a resounding "no" for the following reasons:

1. It is not necessary

You can be well prepared for your bar exam in six weeks or less, while taking plenty of breaks. If you do not have to start studying earlier, why should you?

2. You may run out of gas

The bar exam is a marathon, not a race. If you start too soon, you may run out of steam when bar exam week arrives.

3. You may develop bad bar exam habits

The bar exam is not a law school exam. If you approach it the same, you may falter. And, if you start studying before your bar prep program tells you start, you may study incorrectly or in a manner that is not the most effective. Thus, you will have wasted time and have to go break the bad habits you just started developing.

4. Bar prep programs don't tell you to

If a bar prep program does not tell you to start earlier, then why are you doing it? Their entire business model is based on helping you pass, and if they do not foresee you passing by starting earlier, then why are you doing it?

5. You might forget the earlier stuff

The bar exam is all about retention. At the end of the day, if what you are doing is not helping you retain information for bar exam week, it is all for naught, and you just might forget what you studied three months ago.

6. You might freak out

A big mistake I made was to use my bar exam materials to study for my last law school final in Remedies. When I read a bar exam essay question and sample answer, I froze in fear because it was so different than what I was learning in class, and I got really scared about the bar exam. I shut that book as if it were the board game Jumanji and didn't open it until I had my bar prep program as my guide and mentor.

Exceptions to not starting early

Like all bar exam rules, there are always exceptions:

1. You will be working

If you will be working and just will not have enough time to prepare during normal bar season, then start early if you desire.

2. You are a foreign-trained attorney

Start going through the materials to at least get accustomed to the American format and writing style. If you can, go look at sample answers and just practice writing the sample answer over and over to improve your writing ability and get an idea of how American writing flows.

Best way to use early time

If you are just dying to start studying early, then just thumb through the materials. But, I don't recommend you do MBE questions nor start memorizing rules. Again, it's a waste of time without the proper mentorship.

On the other hand, if you can hit the bar exam prep with your mindset ready to rock, that would be a great use of your time! I highly recommend you spend your energies getting your mindset and lifestyle ready to go.   That means apply the suggestions in Step 2 and Step 3. Get your routine set, start reading your affirmations and bar exam script, and use the techniques from the Bar Exam Mental Edge.

FAQ #2
What materials should I focus on studying and what can I Ignore?

Whether you are in a bar prep program or not, you probably have a lot of materials you could be studying. The problem is that more is not better. More just creates anxiety. The key is to focus on the materials that will best help you pass the bar, not those which give very little return on the time you invest in it.

This is one of the biggest problems bar students face. Generally, bar prep programs do not provide a good solution because they are often the ones that create the problem in the first place with material overwhelm. It took me awhile to figure out the answer to this question, but people have praised me for the advice I am about to give you.

Let's take a bird's eye look at everything you could be doing. In a nutshell, it looks like this:

- Attending bar prep lectures
- Reviewing bar prep lecture notes
- Reading outlines to memorize rules
- Taking timed and untimed practice essays, MBE, and performance tests

- Making flash cards
- Making attack sheets

That is pretty much all you could possibly be doing to prepare for your bar exam. Let us look at each item to determine what the return on time investment will be.

1. Attending bar prep lectures – Yes, do it

In my bar prep lectures, we had two types of lectures: 1) Content lectures and 2) Strategy lectures. The content lectures were just a massive review of the topic. The strategy lectures were a tactical guide to each subject.

Attending Content lectures can be helpful, but they are not the best use of your time. However, I still recommend you do attend your lectures simply because of the "Onion" concept I mentioned earlier. It is good to hear the material again, and to do so from the perspective of the bar exam. Also, you may be writing notes while in lecture, and the writing process itself helps you get acquainted with and remember the material.

On the other hand, attending Strategy lectures is an absolute must. This is where you learn how to pass the bar exam. These are the tricks, tips, and techniques you learn that actually make the bar prep program useful. It was the strategy lectures that taught me that 75% of Evidence questions are on

Character, Hearsay, and Impeachment. These lectures taught me that 25% of Con Law MBE questions will be on the 1st Amendment. By the way, I give a whole long list of these tips I got from my bar prep program in my bonus chapter. Don't miss it!

2. Reviewing lecture notes – No, don't do it

Unless you are reviewing your notes in the context of actually doing practice tests, this activity will be a big waste of time. I started my prep doing lots of class note review until I learned that it did not at all help me do better on my essays or MBE.

I actually spent three days in a row reviewing about 150 contracts hypothetical questions we learned in my bar prep class. The hypotheticals were very good and I figured if I mastered them, I would be able to crush any contracts question that came my way. I did nothing else during those three days, and when my moment of truth came, I did a contracts MBE practice test only to quickly find myself crying (figuratively, although I did cry at least once during my bar prep).

I missed four out of my first five questions. The essay was not any better. I looked at the essay and had no idea what to do. In effect, I wasted three days of bar prep and fell so far behind, I would never catch up to where I was supposed to be.

But, in all failure there is a lesson. Thankfully, this happened early on so I could learn from it. It was then that I realized the class notes, outlines, and rote memorization were all just a waste of time.

What I ultimately needed to do was learn how to do well on the essays and MBE under timed, practice conditions. After all, that's what we are actually tested on, right? We are not tested on the language of the rules or hypothetical situations.

Thus, unless you are going to look at your notes to figure out something you saw on an essay or MBE question, skip this activity. You will save hours of time, headache, and energy.

3. Read outlines to memorize rules – No, don't do it

Going into my bar prep I thought this would be the most important thing I had to do. It was also recommended by my bar prep program to read our outline of rules (called the Conviser) before each class.

Reading rules is a huge waste of time for the following reasons:
- You don't remember any rules after reading them anyway
- It takes a lot of time and energy to get through
- It is extremely boring
- It does not help you do better on your exams or MBE

- With limited time and energy, this activity has a low return on time investment

If you just want to become acquainted with the material, then breeze through the rules or go to your class lecture on the topic. If you want to memorize rules, the best way is take practice tests and look at sample answers to see how the sample answer worded and used the rule. If you are a flash card person, then make your flash cards.

Myth-Buster
"I need to know all the rules to pass."
The rules are actually a very small graded portion of your essays. 60-70% of your points come from your analysis, while 20-30% from the rule statements. Even if you get the wrong rule, you can still get partial points with a good analysis. I have even seen a 65 passing essay that had only one rule statement in the entire essay! It also had great analysis. The real key is to spot the issue and apply the facts.

4. **Take timed and untimed practice essays, MBE, and performance tests – Heck yes, do it!**

I promise you, this is the <u>absolute best use of your time</u>, if you do it correctly. Now you are getting into the meat and potatoes of the bar exam. You are actually preparing for the exact thing you will be tested on. I go in detail about the best approach to these areas later in this chapter, as well as in Steps 5 and Steps 6 of the book. For now, know that the more practice exams you take, the better off you will be. That is a promise.

5. Making flash cards – If you want to

Personally, I think this is a waste of time. However, I know people learn and understand differently. It is more important for you to learn and study the way you feel most comfortable than to not make flash cards because I said so. If you were a flash card person in law school, then stay a flash card person for the bar exam.

Quick Tip
Stick with the same study habits you had in law school. Using the system you are most comfortable with will benefit you the most. If you studied in groups, used flash cards, made long outlines, etc., then continue doing the same.

6. Making attack sheets – Yes, do it

An attack sheet is a list of issues that could come up on the bar exam. Attack sheets are different than outlines. Outlines are a long list of rules. Attack sheets are a long checklist of issues to look for in your essay. This is critical to have. Some people like to make long outlines that eventually condense down to an attack sheet. Some people like to buy their attack sheets online.

I made my own attack sheets because I needed it to be in a system or format that I could best comprehend and analyze for each essay that came up. Usually, there is a mnemonic to memorize.

For example, with torts, part of your attack sheet might be "BAFTTN…" which stands for "Battery, Assault, False Imprisonment, Trespass to chattels, Trespass to Property, Negligence, etc." Thus, when you see a torts question and you want to make sure you have all the issues spotted, you just go down your checklist of possible issues that could be raised.

Making attack sheets are a work in progress during the entire bar prep process. I did not have my attack sheets finalized until a few days before the exam, and I did not have one for every topic. If you go about studying the essays, naturally you will develop a good system for you to spot the issues effectively. Mine happened to be an attack sheet.

There you have it. If you go to your lectures and dig right on into the practice tests, you will save so much time and energy and be so far ahead in preparation from the rest, it will be ridiculous. You will be relaxing on the beach with a week to go from bar prep and no one will be able to figure out why you are so relaxed and how you got so far ahead. Just send them a link to my book, and I'll do all the explaining for you ☺.

FAQ #3
In what order should I study my bar exam materials?

Now that we got rid of the time wasting activities of rote rule memorization and reviewing lecture notes, let's look at the order of attack.

In general, here is the way I *started* out my bar prep early on:

1) Read outline of topic
2) Go to class lecture on topic
3) Review class notes on topic
4) Do untimed 17-question MBE on topic
5) Review every MBE answer, regardless of right or wrong
6) If you did well on prior MBE, do another 17-question MBE on topic, but under timed conditions. If you did not do well on prior MBE, do another untimed 17-question MBE on topic.
7) Do 1 untimed practice essay
8) Review 1 untimed practice essay and try to do it again.
9) Do another untimed practice essay on topic and review it again
10) Do timed practice essays and review answer
11) Do timed practice MBE's and review answer

Through the bar exam struggles, here is what I figured out:

1) ~~Read outline of topic~~
2) Go to class lecture on topic
3) ~~Review class notes on topic~~
4) Do untimed 17-question MBE on topic
5) Review every MBE answer, regardless of right or wrong
6) If I did well on prior MBE, I would do another 17-question MBE on topic, but under timed conditions. If I did not do well on prior MBE, I would do another untimed 17-question MBE on topic.
7) Do 1 untimed practice essay
8) Review 1 untimed practice essay and try to do it again.
9) Do another untimed practice essay on topic and review it again
10) Do timed practice essays and review answer
11) Do timed practice MBE's and review answer

As I said in FAQ #2, I got rid of the 1st and 3rd activity. So, what I recommend is this:

1. Start with your class lecture

Go to class and listen to the lecture on the topic to get an overview of what is going on.

2. Go straight into an <u>untimed</u> 17-question practice MBE

After the lecture, do this before trying to learn or memorize any rules. Go one question at a time and review the answer to each question as you do it.

Read the answer carefully to see why the right answer is the right answer and why the wrong answers are the wrong answers. Do this same process for all 17 questions. I use 17 questions because that is what was provided in my booklet. If you have more or less that is ok, but make it around 17 to start off with.

I recommend starting with the MBE before the essays because the MBE is largely rule-based, and it is easier to start learning the rules and how they work by going through an MBE test.

3. Either re-take the same MBE again or do another <u>untimed</u> practice MBE

After you did all 17 questions above, either go back and re-take the MBE again in full to see if you can get all the right answers, knowing the reason why it is right. Or you can just move on to a second, 17-question MBE.

The reason you might go back and do it again is to ingrain it into your mind and build up your confidence that you know the answers and can do it. Of course, since you just saw the questions, you will probably remember all the answers, so it will not be much of a challenge. However, the process of going through it, knowing why you are picking the answer, and getting it right starts to build a solid foundation of success in your mind. So, experiment with re-doing the same MBE or moving onto another one.

Also, do not time yourself on these. You are learning the material right now, so don't add the pressure of time just yet. Further, take note of the rules that are given in the answers. These are your first glance at them, and they will be the same rules you use in your essays.

Take your time with this. After all, this is your version of learning the material and 'memorizing the rules' that others are spending countless hours on. Except you are actually learning <u>how to apply</u> the rules; whereas, everyone else is just <u>learning</u> the rules. They will then have to learn how to apply them later. You are getting two things done at once! Booya!

4. Do a Timed MBE or do an <u>untimed</u> practice essay

After two MBE tests, by now you have probably spent a few hours on the MBE. If you are getting tired of doing it, then move onto the essays and come back later to do a timed MBE. Otherwise, just jump straight into a timed MBE.

Don't do more than two <u>untimed</u> MBE's. After two, you should be ready to start timing yourself. That does not mean you will necessarily pass the MBE, but it is a good point to start adding a little time pressure.

Remember, this is all practice so who gives a dang if you are failing right now! That is the point! It is not failure, you are learning. I am not saying that to be nice. You are actually <u>not</u> failing because you are learning. Go review each answer as you go through, whether you got it right or wrong.

While others are still looking at rules, they have not even got on the court yet. You are on the basketball court working your butt off right now, while they are still in the backroom reading on what arm motion is to be used when shooting a ball. You are ahead of the game, so stick with it.

<u>When doing a Timed MBE:</u>

If you are doing a Timed MBE, you get 1 minute and 48 seconds per question, so do the math. A 17-question MBE should be completed in no more than 30 minutes. Give yourself 60 minutes for a 35-question MBE. Forcing yourself to finish a little sooner is not a bad idea either in order to train you to move a few seconds ahead of schedule.

Go through the MBE all the way <u>without</u> looking at the answers in the back of the book. The point is to get you game ready, and you won't be able to do that during the exam, so do not do it now no matter how tempting it is.

Spend the time to go through it. Afterwards, go and <u>review every single answer</u>, regardless of whether you got it right or wrong. And then double-check with yourself: "If you saw this question again, would you get the right answer?" In your mind or on paper, re-do the question and go through the responses.

Know why you are canceling out some choices and picking others.

These are the rules you should follow for all timed MBE questions. The graders rinse and repeat the same types of questions all the time. If you build this solid block of knowledge and practice as a foundation while you go, do you think there is any way you won't be prepared to pass your MBE?

Also, it is not about the quantity of MBE exams you take, it is the quality of your approach. In my bar prep, we had two big books on the MBE, complete with six short MBE practice question sets per topic. I never made it to the second book and did not need to. A quality review of the first book was all that I needed using the method just described.

Practice essays

It is so important to start doing practice essays *untimed* because you are simply <u>learning</u> the material right now, not testing yourself.

Quick Tip
Even if you plan on typing the exam, practice at least one handwritten essay and one performance test. No one anticipates a computer error, but every year it happens to someone. If you go through the process of writing out an essay by hand, then you will feel more confident, if that rare situation should occur. Also, make sure you are not using an old computer, which could be prone to crashing!

<u>1st practice essay</u>

Regardless of whether you actually spend time learning the law or not, I guarantee you will fail your first essay miserably. That is perfectly awesome. Say it with me... Awesome. Here is how I recommend you approach your <u>first</u> essay.

1. Do a 10- to 15- minute outline

Spend ten to fifteen minutes reading the essay and try to make an outline as best as you can. No matter what, spend only that block of time. No more, no less, for now. What are the possible issues? What factors do you remember from the class lecture or law school that determine the outcome of those issues. Which facts seem relevant? Since you will be way off and probably not spot even half of the issues, only spend ten to fifteen minutes doing an outline on this.

2. Look at the sample answer

Take a look at the sample answer. Which issues does it show? What facts are relevant? Spend some time looking at it and reading through it. Even start memorizing some of the rules they used. By the way, <u>this is how and when I recommend you actually spend time memorizing rules and learning the law</u>. This would be the time to reference your copious notes and outline, in the specific context of the issue you are working.

3. Go back and do the essay untimed

Now, that you have seen the answer, can you duplicate it? Go back and re-read the question and try to do the essay as if you were looking at it fresh. By doing this now, you will at least have an idea of what issues are present, what the rules are, and what facts are relevant. Go through and outline the essay, then write it out in full.

This will be different than when you reviewed your MBE. In your MBE re-take, you probably remembered all the answers. For the essay, you will not! It will surprise you how you go back and re-take the essay moments after you saw the answer and you still don't remember all the issues, rules, factors, or facts that were used.

That is ok. It is part of the learning process and this is the absolute best way to learn how to pass the essays! Now, you have tried to spot issues and write rules, but you got it wrong.

4. Go back and compare the sample answer to your answer

After writing out a full answer, go back and look at the sample answer again and compare it to your answer. This time, you probably got most of it right, but still missed a few things. Figure out what it was and you may even want to rewrite just that portion of the test to practice writing the rule and using it in the context of an exam.

By doing this, you have now gone over this essay several times and if you ever see any of these issues or rules again (which you will), you will know how to handle them now!

2nd practice essay

Do the same thing you did on the first practice essay. You will probably fail this one miserably as well, but just go through the same process and learn the issues, rules, factors, and what facts are relevant.

3rd practice essay

Do the full one hour on this essay immediately. You will probably do 10 times better. You may actually pass this essay. By the time I did my third essay, half the time, I was actually passing it! Can you believe it? Two essays in and now you are passing the essays! How is that possible when you haven't done any rote rule memorization?

It is possible because the bar exam graders rinse and repeat all the time. The same group of issues will come up on the bar exam all the time. Now that you have seen two essays, you will probably run into many similar issues on the third essay. Because you went over it, reviewed them in the prior essays, and created a foundation of applicable knowledge, you can handle them well now.

It is genius, I know! You might not get all the issues, but you will probably get most of them. By the time you do the 4th essay and 5th essay, you should be money in the bank and knocking these essays out of the park. Make your third essay and all others after that a timed essay.

From here on out, just do a combination of timed MBE and timed essays tests. You have the foundation, so now it is just time to practice, practice, and do more practice. Do the full timed test. Don't just outline the essays. For those of you taking performance tests, use the same techniques I described in the essays.

Quick Tip
Start your bar prep with your topics that also cover the MBE. Then, you will be killing two birds with one stone right off the bat, when you are fresh. If you spend three days per topic to start out, you will have reviewed the entire MBE and half your essays within the first three weeks of bar prep!

Myth-Buster
"If I have low MBE scores, I should work harder on the essays to make up for it."
Wrong. If you are scoring low on the MBE, getting higher essay scores will not help you make up for it. The exam is curved, so it will be harder to score higher on the essays anyway. The goal should be to pass each section, not try and skid by overall by doing extra well in one section. If you have low MBE scores, focus on improving them. If you have low essay scores, focus on improving those. Treat each section of the exam separate and equal (Con Law shout out!).

Repeater Tip
If you are a repeater and passed the essays the first time, don't just ignore them and only do the MBE the second time around. You passed the essays because you put in time for the essays and will need to do so again. It works the same if you passed the MBE and only think you should put in time on the essays.

FAQ #4
How many Essays, MBE questions, and PT's should I do?

There is no single right answer to this question. It depends on how well you are doing, your prior experience with writing and taking multiple choice tests, and how comfortable you are with the material. Although the answer varies per person, there is a general opinion I have based on the bar exam talk going around and my own personal experience.

As an average, I recommend you do at least the following amounts:
- Do 100-150 MBE questions per topic, with in-depth review
- Take 6 timed practice essays per topic, with in-depth review
- Take 4 timed Performance tests, with in-depth review

Some people do more and some do less. I believe these numbers are relatively lower compared to what most other people do, and I do believe I spent less time studying than others.

The reason is because I learned more is not better. It is not about the <u>number</u> of practice exams you do, but the <u>effectiveness</u> of the practice exams that you do. If you follow the system I outlined above in FAQ#3, you will see that is a very effective approach. I am not breezing through practice exams to get on to the next. I spent my time with each one learning the intricacies of it because I believe that is the best way.

If you follow my approach above, then doing this amount per topic area should get you well and ready to pass your bar exam.

Quick Tip
These are suggestions I give based on my own experience and the observations of others. Ultimately, you must study in the method that you learn the best. These methods will not work the best for everyone, but I do encourage you to try them.

FAQ #5
How many hours per day should I study?

Again, there is no right answer to this question. It depends on whether you are working, how efficient you are, and the effectiveness of what you are studying. It is not really the number of hours you spend, but *what you are doing during those hours.*

Ten hours of memorizing rules for torts will not prepare you in the same way as ten hours of doing practice essays for torts. The former will hardly get you ready to pass, but the latter definitely will.

Your energy levels are important too. Eight hours of studying when you are hungry and sleep-deprived will be far less effective than a person who spends only six hours, but ate a good meal, exercised, and did 30 minutes of outdoor meditation.

Try not to focus on number of hours. Instead, focus on 1) Actual activities you are studying and accomplishing and 2) Having good, healthy energy while you study. If you have those two in place, you will be light years ahead of everyone else. I promise. Now that I emphasized the importance of those two points, I will go ahead and answer your question.

Let us first look at all the tasks we would have to do, then calculate the hours spent per task. These hours are very approximate and are at the ideally high end, assuming you do all that I recommend and you do it perfectly. I didn't even do what I recommend to do perfectly. But, let's have some fun and take a look.

a) *Essays:*

If I am doing six timed practice essays and a couple untimed essays, that will be about eight hours of doing essays. If I spend about 30 minutes reviewing each essay, then another 30 to 60 minutes re-taking each essay, that is about 16 hours of essay practice per topic maximum.

These are not numbers I actually spent. I may have spent less time reviewing some and more time reviewing others. Also, I did not always go back and re-take timed essays, although I did review them. Furthermore, I did not always do six essays per topic. To maintain my energy or if I understood the material well enough, sometimes I only did two or three essays per topic. I recommended the six above because if you can do it, you will be very well prepared.

Let's say that you do about 15 hours of essays per topic multiplied by 12 topic areas = 180 hours. That would be ideal. In reality, on average, it will probably be closer to 120 hours.

b) *MBE:*

If you do 100 to 150 MBE questions per topic, that is about five hours of doing MBE questions. Then, do another ten or so hours of thorough review. That is 15 hours multiplied by 6 topics = 90 hours of MBE practice.

Again, this is ideal. I did not do 150 per topic, although I probably came close. On average, it will probably be closer to 70 hours of MBE practice.

c) *Performance Tests:*

The timing of these depends on your jurisdiction. I did about four full performance tests and outlined three more. With review, let us say about 25 hours at the high end for doing performance tests.

d) *Class Lectures:*

In Bar/Bri, we had about seven weeks of lectures, four hours per day, about five or six days per week. That averages out to be about 150 hours.

e) *Memorizing and reviewing Rules, Notes, Attack Sheets:*

I learned not to put as much emphasis on this outside of practice tests. Let us say about four or five hours per the twelve topics, which is about 50 hours.

Thus, we have about:

- Essays   120 to 180 hours
- MBE   70 to 90 hours
- Performance Tests   25 hours
- Lectures   150 hours
- Memorizing   50 hours

That is about 425 - 500 hours of total studying, at the ideally high end. After class lectures, that is about 275 hours of studying. If you spent 50 days (seven weeks) studying, that is about five or six hours of studying outside class lectures per day, which is not too bad.

Again, this is an ideal average. I can't say definitively how much time I spent because I did not clock in and out as if I were at a billable law firm. Also, remember it is about 1) what you are actually doing, and 2) your energy while you do it. This has been a fun way to budget your time and see how much time preparing for the bar exam might take.

Myth-Buster
"Do I really have to study 10 hours everyday?"
Of course not. If you can focus on the needle-movers, like practice tests, you significantly reduce the amount of time you spend studying and make yourself much more prepared. More hours is not better. Work smart and energized hours, not long hours. Also, periodic breaks and occasional day-long breaks are a necessity to maintain mental focus and energy.

Quick Tip
Make sure you focus on improving your weak areas. Do not just practice your strong areas over and over. Thus, if you have torts down, but are weak in contracts, make sure you are spending a lot of time practicing contracts. If you are good on the MBE, but weak on the PT's, make sure you put in more practice on the PT's.

Quick Tip

Want some more tips from different perspectives? Be sure to check out the following bar exam blogs:

- *http://IPassedMyBarExam.com ← That's me!*
- *http://BarExamToolbox.com*
- *http://MindOverBar.com*
- *http://BeAGoat.com*
- *http://BarExamMind.com*
- *http://CaliforniaGbx0707.blogspot.com/*

STEP FIVE
The 11 Keys to Passing the Bar Essays

The essays are the largest graded portion of your bar exam and will take the most time and effort. Here are the 11 keys to passing your essays:

1. Take lots of practice essays, under timed conditions

As I stated in Step 1 and Step 4 above, the key to passing is practice. The only thing you will be asked on exam day is to review a fact pattern, spot the issues, apply the rules, and use the facts in one hour. The best way to prepare for that day is to ... Get a fact pattern, spot the issues, apply the rules and use the facts in one hour. If you are only outlining essays, not timing yourself, or doing other activities, you are lessening your preparation.

Myth-Buster
"I can just outline essay answers and get by because I will know how to analyze on the actual test."
Do so at your own peril. Outlining and writing are two very different activities and skill sets. Although, outlining allows you to go through many essays and is great for developing your issue-spotting ability, combine that with doing plenty of practice actually writing out the essays. The writing process will help

you write rules, analyze, develop your timing skills, and truly get you game-ready.

2. Practice your Issue Spotting

Issue spotting, not rule statements, are the most important component of your essay skills to develop. If you do not spot the issue, you won't get the points. This technique cannot be practiced enough. Here are six ways to increase your issue-spotting ability:

a) *Have an attack sheet*

Have a long list of possible issues that could come up for any given topic. If you commit this to memory, no essay will stand a chance against you. Just go through each potential issue and ask yourself, "Is this issue at all relevant in this essay?" If it may even be remotely relevant, mention it, even if it is just a sentence or two. For example:

"There is no battery because A did not make physical contact with B."

b) *Why Why Why? Test*

If everything happens for a reason, then certainly every fact in an essay is there for a reason. Go through each fact and ask yourself, 'why why why?' is this fact here? Why is it a "speeding" vehicle? Why did the fact pattern mention "at night"? Essay fact patterns are like poetry. No word goes in without a purpose. Often times, even if you have no idea about what issues are presented on a fact pattern, by working backwards and looking at the specific words and facts, you will be lead to what issues are being presented.

c) New paragraph in the fact pattern typically means a new issue

In congruence with the 'why why why?' test, why are there new paragraphs in the fact pattern? Is the grader trying to be nice on your eyes? I doubt it. Many times a new paragraph will equal a new issue. If you are having trouble spotting an issue, just look for the new paragraph.

d) Something sounds fishy?

By the time you have read hundreds of rules and practiced dozens of essays, your sense of justice will be very high. In the fact pattern, if something just does not sound fair or right, then it is probably an issue. If a person should be punished for an act, but you cannot quite figure out why or what, just start writing about it because there is probably an issue there.

e) Use your law school knowledge

You did spend three or so years in law school reading cases and doing final exams right? Bring those skills you already have to the table!

f) Start writing

Sometimes, when you just start writing, things open up and you spot the issues.

Quick Tip
If you think there might be an issue at play, talk about it. The bar graders don't penalize you for writing more. They will just ignore it. Just make sure it fits neatly into your organized answer.

3. Write short, direct, clear, and concise analysis

Don't be a rambler. I spent my entire law school being a rambler, which is why I did poorly on many exams. I would do many counter arguments, almost as if I were facilitating a debate discussion. I completely changed my writing style for the bar exam and learned to be short, concise, and to the point. Boring and direct is highly encouraged on the bar exam.

It would be very good to check out your state bar website and look at the model answers just to see how direct and to the point the answers are. Don't worry. You don't have to write that well overall, but it will give you some insight on how short analysis really should be. I have seen several model answer essays with only one or two sentences of analysis per issue. Generally speaking, that is how your answer should look.

An example of how analysis should look

Go to the California bar website, pull up the February 2010, 1ˢᵗ model answer. Notice how concise the wording is. There is basically only a one sentence rule per paragraph. Look at the issue, rule, and analysis used on Page 5. First is the clearly defined issue:

> "Danco claims that Pat anticipatorily repudiated the contract when he called on the 15ᵗʰ of April saying, —I won't have it ready to deliver to you until at least May 8th—maybe closer to May 15."

Next is the one-sentence rule:

> "A contract is anticipatorily repudiated when a party unequivocally manifests an intention to not perform the agreement by words or conduct."

Now read the analysis:

> "Here, although the contract specified performance by the 1ˢᵗ of May, Pat indicated that he would perform at least half of the services by that time, and indicated he would complete the other two within a couple weeks."

That is the <u>entire</u> analysis for that rule. It is a one-sentence statement that only repeats the facts.

Notice there are no fancy, cute, long, or clever arguments.

Then, the answer concludes:

> "Thus, he did not unequivocally manifest an intention to not perform the contract, but merely requested an extension of time, or modification of the contract. Thus, Danco could not treat the contract as breached but could ask for assurances that the contract would be performed."

The same applies in the next paragraph. Take a look and break it down:

- 1st sentence – Restates the issue
- 2nd sentence – One Line Rule
- 3rd sentence – One Fact
- 4th sentence – One rule
- 5th sentence – Conclusion
- 6th sentence – Rule/Conclusion

The answer used only one fact again and sandwiched it in between two rules. Do you see how concise, direct, and short these answers are? And it is a model answer on the California bar website.

Quick Tip
Generally, your essay answer should be no more than three pages. If you write too much or your essay is too long, it will send a red flag signal to the grader.

It would be a great idea for you to go through other model answers on your state bar website and next to each sentence, write out if the sentence is either an 1) issue, 2) rule, 3) analysis, or 4) conclusion. This will help you see how the really good answers are broken down, so you can apply the same techniques.

4. Spend at least 15 minutes outlining before you write your answer

This is another skill I had to develop for my bar exam. I never outlined in law school (and I wonder why my grades were poor). Time and time again, Bar/Bri preached the importance of outlining, so I fell in line and learned the skill. It is a very good thing I did so.

The bar exam fact patterns are much shorter than what you see in law school. They are typically only one page long fact patterns, compared to three, four, or even five pages in law school.

Thus, organization is so important on the bar exam. This is another reason why you cannot treat your law school exams the same as your bar exam.

In my law school pre-bar prep class, we had a bar tutor come and speak to us. The tutor would only coach repeat examinees in California and was 50-0 in having his repeat students pass the California bar exam. Not a single failure!

He told us that out of all the repeaters who came to him for help, not a single one of them outlined during their bar exam. That means 50 people took the bar exam and did not outline their essays. All 50 of those failed.

How to outline:

Outlining is actually really easy and methodical. You take each fact in the fact pattern and parse it out. If this fact were relevant to an issue (which it almost always will be), what issue would it be relevant to? Then, what factor in that issue would it be relevant to?

If in the fact pattern you see:

"During a game of bouncy ball at recess, A threw a rubber ball intending to hit B in the face, but instead hit C. C started crying and later got scars on his face."

Then your outline would be something like this:

C vs. A

Battery
- Intent
  - No because A did not intend to hit C
  - Transferred intent – A attempted to hit C, thus intent transferred to anyone who contact is made with, thus this element is satisfied

- Contact
  - Yes, because the ball hit C

- Harmful/offensive
  - Maybe, C would argue he was harmed by the contact because of the scars and it made him cry.
  - A would argue that the ball was rubber and they were just playing a game

This is in outline format, but in actuality, this is much more writing than you would need for an outline. What I wrote here could fit right into the essay, but you get the idea.

Have your issue with each factor below it. Then dissect the essay by going through each fact, one-by-one, and placing it under an appropriate rule and factor.

15 minute Outline Rule

In reality, on the essays where I really knew what I was doing, I would often spend 20 minutes on my outline. If I was lost, I would only end up spending about ten minutes.

5. Learn to make up rules on the go

This skill was taught to me by my bar prep program and is one of the most important and overlooked skills in all the bar exam. It is the reason why some people fail and many people freak out when they see something they do not know on the bar exam.

In California, you are <u>guaranteed</u> to have at least one essay from completely out of left field. You will look at it and your jaw will drop (in my case, I felt I had a few of these, not just one!). It is the bar examiners' way of testing your composure. They want to see how well you handle yourself. How composed will you be when you see something you do not know and have the pressure of time to get through it?

This will separate a lot of the passers from the re-takers. The key is not to freak out about it, but rather to prepare for it. The bar examiners very well know the question is coming from left field, and they know the average score will be far less on that answer. Remember, if you do not know it, nobody knows it!

The best way to prepare for this is practicing making up rules and issues when you are not sure what is going on. To do that, you must <u>take practice essays</u>, under <u>timed conditions</u> and <u>complete them no matter what</u>.

When you freak out during practice and force yourself to finish anyway, you are learning a valuable skill of finishing. You are learning to take the closed universe of the fact pattern and figure out what issue may be present and what rule sounds reasonable. The only way to do that is to actually practice doing that when the pressure is on during practice.

Try it and see. I guarantee you that sometimes you will be shocked by how close your 'made-up' issues and rules are to the actual answer. That happened to me several times and gave me a lot of confidence to know that I can handle myself even when I don't quite understand the fact pattern. I can make it through. After all, I don't need an A on this essay. I just need a D. If I can skate through with a D, that is all good for me.

After you finish the practice essay, then go back and look at the answer. Learn what it really is and re-write your answer so you ingrain it into your mind.

By the way, did you know that you get partial points even if you use the wrong rule? Put the wrong rule and apply the facts to the wrong rule and you get partial points from the graders! The reason is because they know you will not know every single rule in the book. They know as a lawyer you are going to look up the rules anyway. They really want to test your deductive reasoning and logic skills. Can you make sense of an essay fact pattern? Can you decipher the injustices going on and apply some logic and reason to the fact pattern? That is all they really want in the end.

In addition, by making up the rule, you may get half of it or even the whole rule correct. You won't lose any points for adding it in, and the bar graders may not even notice during their frantic three minute read of your essay.

How this technique made me a bar exam passer

Rewind to the February 2010 California bar exam, Day 3, Essay number 2. I open my booklet and I see an entire question about Con Law – Takings. Holy crapola. I did not once do an essay on this topic. I may have looked at the rule once months before. I had no idea how to go about it.

Well, it is a good thing I learned the skill I am preaching here. I made up my own "Saiidi 4-part test" to determine whether there was a government taking or not (I did not actually call it 'Saiidi' on the exam).

By this time, I had read so many rules, I was actually pretty good at playing judge and making up a set of rules on the go. I have no idea how I scored on that essay, which is a good thing because that is what happens when you pass the bar exam!

So, just practice as I stated above in Step 4 and do the essays under timed conditions, through to completion. Remember it is just practice, you are just learning, and no one else has to see your score. No need to be fearful about it.

6. Write like a lawyer

I told you in the introduction, my writing grades in law school were some of my worst. In my bar prep program, they assumed you already knew how to write and had very little emphasis on how to improve your writing skill.

Many people will do everything proper in preparation, but their writing is not concise and clear like a lawyer would be expected to write. Bar prep programs do not really help you with this component. You can get help by going to a tutor or do what I did.

I went into the sample essays in the back of the Bar/Bri essay book. I looked at the samples and literally re-typed them out, word for word. I did this several times and quickly noticed the more professional and succinct grammar and sentence structure. I only had to do this for a few essays before I understood and incorporated this method of writing into my own essays. Others have done this too, and it worked for them. So, try it! If you do not have that book, just get your hands on a good sample answer to copy from your bar website or Bar Essays.

7. Underline, use Headings, and have plenty of white space

Bar exam graders are human beings, not machines. Adam Ferber, the former head of bar exam graders in California, reported that bar graders likely suffer from the 'Blink' effect, as discussed in Malcolm Gladwell's famous book.

Ferber stated that when a bar grader first opens up your exam, he will make an immediate snap judgment about your exam based on how it looks. Is it filled with long paragraphs? Or are there headings indicating new issues? Are there underlined topics and important facts? Is there plenty of white space that makes the exam more readable?

If you have the latter setup, you might pass that essay even if it is not the best essay! If the former, you are very unlikely to pass even if you do have all that is needed.

This fact was also verified by Gil Peles of BarEssays in the podcast interview I did with him. After reviewing thousands of essays, he found that even answers that had all the 'right stuff' failed because the grader likely got lost in the mess and could not follow in a logical, succinct manner.

Whether they know it or not, the graders will take this snap judgment and filter everything else they read in your essay based on it. It is like a job interview. You might be Zuckerberg-intelligent, but if you show up to the interview with sweats and t-shirt on, the interviewer won't hire you despite the brilliance you may exhibit.

Does this sound fair? It may or may not be, but the bottom line is that it is happening. You need to have an organized looking essay answer or you are asking for failure, rendering everything else you study useless.

Remember the purpose of the bar exam? It is to pass the bar exam, that is it! So do what the graders want. Use this knowledge to your advantage. It is so easy to do. Just underline new issue headings you write, have a new paragraph after the rule, and another one after the analysis and you are on your way to impressing the graders!

Still do not believe me? Go to the model answer for your state bar. Almost all the model answers will probably have headings and plenty of white space.

Perhaps it is fair to grade this way. Lawyers are supposed to be organized and clear in their writing, are they not? What is unfair is that very few people will tell you the importance of this component. People think it is all about memorizing the rules. As you see now, it is about more than that.

Quick Tip

Did you know, on average, graders only spend three minutes grading your essay? If they cannot find what they need to find in three minutes time, they will move on to the next. They don't have time nor patience to look for it.

Follow these few rules when drafting good headings:

1. Draw attention to headings

You can draw attention to them by following these three simple rules. I recommend you use them in this order of importance:

1. Underlined – This will be the most noticeable.
2. Bold

3. Capitalized – Not necessary, but a nice touch. If you have the headings bold and underlined, you don't need to capitalize.

2. Keep it concise

The headings are concise statements. They should be short, direct, and sweet.

3. Word them optimally

I have heard conflicting views on how to word the headings. In actuality, it probably does not matter much, but here they are. Bar/Bri recommends just stating the issue, like "Battery." Adam Ferber recommends you give a summarized statement, as opposed to one word. For a heading, do not write:

Battery

> **Intent**
> **Contact**
> **Harmful or offensive**

Instead, state:

B committed Battery on A

> **B had the requisite INTENT required**
> **B made PHYSICAL CONTACT with A**
> **B's contact was OFFENSIVE**

These headings signal to the grader that you know the issue, the elements, and it's likely to be more logical, thorough, and organized. On the other hand, Gil has noticed that essays, which are formatted in this C-RAC form instead of I-RAC, tend to score lower. I used the Bar/Bri method, and it seemed to work fine for me. Pick how you like!

8. Use actual statute numbers

Bar exam prep programs tell you that it is not necessary to use actual code numbers on your bar exam. Perhaps it is not; however, Gil has noticed that essays that do use code numbers tend to score five to ten points higher than similar essays which do not use the numbers.

It comes down to the 'Blink' effect again. If you are so impressive as to be using actual statute numbers, the grader will think you know what you are talking about and is more likely to grade you favorably.

You don't need the code numbers for all topics, but when talking about the following sections, definitely use the code numbers in your answer:

- FRE 403
- CA Evidence Code 352
- Proposition 8
- State "Under the 4th amendment," not "Under search and seizure rules"

9. Do not guess what essay topics will be tested

Unless you have super good instincts which you trust, do not listen to predictions about which topic will be covered and which will not. Predicting Super Bowl champions is easier than predicting which essays will be covered, and I even predicted a 49er-Patriot Super Bowl 47 at the beginning of the season (so close to happening)! Just prepare for all the topics and do not mess around with vague predictions.

10. Spend no more than 1 hour per essay

This is a golden rule. Get into the habit of spending one hour and only one hour on each of your essays. People think spending more time on one essay will get them significantly more points that will make up for other essays. This is simply not true.

The exam is on a graded curve. A good hour spent might get you a 65 or a 70 on an essay. If you spent another 15 minutes, then you *might* go up to a 70 or 75. That is 15 minutes of work for 5 points. Now, you have only 45 minutes for your next essay. 45 minutes on that essay might get you a 50 or a 55. That is 10 to 15 points less than what you would have received. Thus, you have cost yourself valuable points.

In my interview with Gil, he says just as much. He has seen people getting as high as an 80 on the first essay and a zero on their 3rd essay. There is no coming back from a zero. A zero on an essay is like getting shot by the 007 Golden Gun. Game over. Don't risk it. Only one hour per essay. You can listen to our interview at http://IPassedMyBarExam.com/Podcasts.

11. The step-by-step approach to the essays

Here is the best way I learned how to practice each essay.

A) Read the call of the question

Do this <u>before</u> anything else. This is not a novel where you want to be surprised by the ending. Many times, but not always, you can find out what topic the essay will be simply by reading the call of the question. If it is a torts question, you can turn on your 'torts' filter and read everything with that perspective.

Quick Tip
Pay attention to who is suing who. In the example I used above, the call of the question was C v. A. It was not B v. A, which would have been an entirely different analysis. Many times you will see potential causes of action, but you are not asked to analyze them. Many students are caught up in the rush of the moment and don't pay attention, costing them dearly. There is no partial credit for analyzing the wrong parties.

B) Read through the essay once

Just read through it to get an idea of what is going on. If you want, start marking certain elements, but a basic read-through is a good idea at first to get familiar.

C) Write out your attack sheet

Now, that you have a very good idea of what the essay is about, it would be a good time to write out your attack sheet mnemonic – the list of all the possible main issues which can be tested. Write it out on scratch paper in the corner.

For example, with torts, after reading through the fact pattern once, go to the corner of your scratch paper and write: "BAFTTN......" This way you won't forget by blanking out momentarily, and you can easily go through each letter to see if that issue applies or not.

D) Write out the issues and factors in your outline

Then, create your base outline. You probably spotted at least three or four issues that could be at play. Write down 1) Who is suing who, and then 2) the main issue, putting the factors underneath it.

As an example, see the next page.

C v. A
Battery

- Intent

- H/O

- Contact

Assault

- Intent

- Apprehension

Negligence

- Duty

- Breach

- But for causation

- Px

- Damages

- Defenses

    o Comparative liability

    o Etc., etc.,

Make sure to leave some space below each element, so you can easily write down the fact that will be at play there.

> ### E) Read through the essay again carefully, taking each fact and putting it under each element of each issue where it applies.

Example:

C v. A

Battery

- Intent
    - o Facts indicate A intended to hit B
    - o Transferred intent of B to C
- H/O
    - o A – Playing game, not offensive
    - o C – scarred
- Contact
    - o Ball hit

Assault

- Intent
    - o Yes, he tried to hit C
- Apprehension
    - o No facts indicate whether C saw it coming or not
    - o Would need more facts

Negligence

- Duty
    - Duty to not harm others (I am just making stuff up here)

- Breach

- But for causation
    - No harm if did not act

- Px
    - No intervening causes

- Damages
    - Scarred face, harm and crying

- Defenses

    - Comparative liability
        - None in facts

    - Etc., etc.,

F) Read through once more

After you have created a base outline, read through the essay carefully once more to see if you missed anything or for other issues you may not have found.

G) Start writing

If you have a good outline, the writing process is quite simple. It is just plug and play for the next 40-45 minutes.

One of the difficulties with the essays arises when the issues are not clear or you do not recognize all of them. In reality, this will probably happen on at least half of your essays.

If you finish earlier than 1 hour

Whenever I wrote a good essay and spotted all the issues, it would typically take me an hour every time. If I ever finished early, the reason was because I had missed some of the issues.

If this happens to you, do not panic. Just remember your goal is to spot as many issues as you can and give as good an analysis as you can. It is natural to not get every single issue. That is why a grade of a 65 passes, not a 95.

If you finish early or feel like you are missing some of the issues, go back through the issue spotting techniques discussed earlier in this section. Look through your attack sheet again, go through the facts to see what you have not used, look at each new paragraph, and look for something fishy.

If you still cannot find any more issues, make them up

If you do all of that and still cannot recognize any more issues, maybe you got them all already. However, if you ever have a group of facts that have not been used, there is probably an issue hiding there.

Now is the time to make something up. You may have no idea what it is, but it is important to not let any facts go unused. Take that group of facts and try to figure out why the grader would put them. What is the grader trying to signal to you? What injustice is present?

Then make up a short rule that would use the facts and apply the facts. I did this a lot during my practice and several times during my bar exam. Remember, the grader is breezing through your essay in three minutes and you are on his side because you used the 'blink' effect with good headings and white space. The grader may just go through, see that you used the facts, and check off a few positive points for you. Also, you won't get docked for talking about issues that are not present, so extra writing is not bad, so long as it is organized.

See, I told you there is no need to panic! And whoola, you pass the essays.

Quick Tip

The key to this method is to have a good practice essay to review. Don't compare your answers to the state bar model answers. They are ridiculously good, and I never wrote anything that cool-looking. Instead, get a more realistic-looking answer such as the Bar/Bri essay practice book or the graded answers from BarEssays.com.

Myth-Buster

"I can just skim over the Performance tests and figure those out during the bar exam."

The PT's are a large part of your grade. In California, one PT is worth two essays! They do not take as much practice as the essays, but you still want to do several of them fully and completely, under timed conditions. According to Bar/Bri, very few people pass one PT and fail the exam. If you even pass one, that is a good chance of success.

Essay Checklist
- 3 to 4 page answer
- Readable in 3 minutes
- Good Headings
- Lots of clear white space
- Took no more than 1 hour to write
- Went through issue spotting technique checklist
    - o Attack Sheet
    - o Why Why Why
    - o New Paragraph
    - o Fishy?

- Law School knowledge
- Lawyerly Writing

<u>Techniques to Practice and Develop:</u>
- Issue Spotting
- Outlining
- Writing on time
- Making up Rules
- Writing 'lawyerly'

The 7 Steps to Bar Exam Success

STEP SIX
The 8 Keys to Passing the MBE

The MBE is not scored as high as the essays are; however, it is still very important. Do not fool yourself into thinking you can do really well on the essays to make up for low MBE scores and vice versa. Each component needs due time and attention paid to it. Here are eight keys to passing the MBE.

1. Eliminate two answer choices

The MBE is so much about statistics. The more answers you can eliminate, the higher you will score, statistically speaking. It is not true with every question, but generally speaking, you can eliminate two answer choices.

2. One word in the answer makes all the difference

If you think the 'Why Why Why' test was important in the essays, then it is super critical in the MBE. Most of the time, the difference between the right and wrong answer is just in one word. Look for those absolute words like 'never, always' and instead go with the answer that reads, 'often, occasionally.'

3. Focus on the meat and potatoes

There are distinct patterns the bar exam graders consistently follow. Check out my Bar/Bri bonus chapter to get my knowledge of what to look for on the MBE in regards to specific topics and focus your study on those topics. You only need to focus on and eat the meat and potatoes, not everything in the kitchen.

4. Time it out

You have 1 minute and 48 seconds per MBE question. To ensure you are on track with your timing on bar exam day, take your answer sheet and write the following times next to the numbered question. This will let you know what question you should be on when you hit that time period of the exam:

- Question #18 – 30 minutes
- Question #35 – 1 hour
- Question #53 – 1 hour and 30 minutes
- Question #70 – 2 hours
- Question #88 – 2 hours and 30 minutes

This is timed slightly ahead to give you a few extra minutes just in case.

5. Review all your practice answers

When reviewing your answers, make sure you <u>review the questions you got correct</u> and the questions you got incorrect. Sometimes, you are just guessing at a correct question or got it right for the wrong reason. Review why you got it right.

Also, review the reasoning behind <u>all</u> the answer choices. Don't just look at why the answer choice *B* is correct. Determine why choices *A*, *C*, and *D* are incorrect. You do not need to follow these rules with every single test; however, you should do it with most of your tests to be best prepared.

6. Go for a 120 raw score

If you can score a 120 raw score on your MBE, you should be A-ok for passing your exam in any jurisdiction. That would be about an 11/17 or a 23/35 on sample tests.

7. Do not freak out if your scores stop improving past a 120

Many people see improvement in their MBE, then see it stop. They might score a 12 or a 13 out of 17 on their practice and then never a see an improvement beyond that.

Do not freak out if that happens. It is designed to be a curve, and it is extremely difficult to get above a 75% on your MBE practice. If you are in the 11 to 13 range you are doing great! If you are doing it consistently, even better.

8. Do not freak out if your scores start dropping

Sometimes, I would be doing well on the MBE, then another group of tests I would suddenly drop off to 8 or 9 correct out of 17. Initially, I thought I was unlearning or getting dumber, but I realized that is the nature of some of the practice tests. Do not let it mentally affect you. Just keep reviewing and learning as you have been.

STEP SEVEN
The 4 Preparations and 12 Keys to Make bar week your Best Week

With proper preparation, believe it or not you can have a smooth bar exam week. There are four key components to this preparation:

1) Content preparation

This is the prep you do during the bar exam period. There is no way to get around it, and no one passes their bar exam by getting lucky. Content preparation is king and you know that. It is the other stuff that may not be on your radar.

2) Mindset preparation

Some people will know enough and have practiced enough to be ready to knock the bar exam out. However, something may trigger them to go blank once they step into that exam room. It might be the anxious person sitting beside them, the opening of their test booklet, the drive over, etc. I have spoken with test tutors who have seen their students experience this game-time freeze. One little thing can trigger them and send all their prep out the window.

This is the mental component of the bar exam, and it is important to consider and prepare for. This will not necessarily happen to you but sometimes the jitters can get even the best of us. The good news is I will tell you how to mentally prepare yourself for walking into the test room.

Visualize

If you want to truly command your thoughts and emotions, rather than have them command you, spend time during your bar prep visualizing how your bar week is going to go. In your mind, go through the motions of what you are doing the night before, waking up the day of and getting to the test room.

Visualize a peaceful, calm time where you get to the center and everything is going ok. Visualize yourself opening up the answer book and knowing what the right answers are. And visualize yourself walking out each day feeling confident in what you did.

Your mind does not know the difference between reality and imagination. By using your imagination, you, in fact, create your reality. Doing so with your eyes closed in a calm, quiet place will allow you to really focus on what emotions come up and allow you to imagine yourself handling them well and drawing in positive emotions.

Of course, when you get the Bar Exam Mental Edge, I include both a bar Prep and a Bar Week visualization mp3. Each are approximately 20-30 minutes long and walk you through a guided visualization of your bar prep and the bar week.

Affirmations

Use the affirmations and script I gave you in Step 2 of this book. I will send you a printable copy if you go to http://IPassedMyBarExam.com/TheSevenSteps.

Pray

If you have a spiritual or religious faith, this would be a good time to call on it. Realistically, you should be doing this throughout your bar prep, but now is never too late. Pray to do well and also pray for others success on the bar exam. Remember, energy spent returns ten-fold. You are not in competition with anyone but your own doubts.

3) _Logistical preparation_

If you have the mind and content ready to go, then make sure you have all the little ins and outs setup and ready. Here is a checklist of things to keep in mind:

- Have your bar test admission and ID card in an easily reachable place.

- Set two alarms for when you want to wake up and have a friend text or call you as well.

- A week or two before your exam, drive to the test center at the same time of day as your exam to get an idea of traffic patterns, road construction, and any other unforeseen circumstances.

- Survey the parking around the test center and know where you will park, how long you can park there for, if you can pay with cash, etc.

- Have plenty of pens, pencils, and erasers. The test center may have some they give out, but don't count on them.

- Bring only your laptop and charger from your car, not your laptop bag. Some test centers let you place your belongings outside, but don't trust it will still be there when you get back.

- Charge your laptop the night before just in case the outlet is not working at your station.

- Bring a change of clothes. It might be freezing outside and be really hot inside or vice versa. Have a sweatshirt handy with a t-shirt underneath.

- Dress comfortably. I recommend you dress in whatever clothes you wore while preparing. I had a hoodie and jeans.

- Know the restrictions of your center beforehand. Some jurisdictions do not allow hoodies. Some require you wear a suit.

- Bring an approved timer. The test centers are usually really big and they may not have timers for you or it may be too far for you to see. And how can you time yourself without a timer?

- Bring ear plugs if you want to. I was never an ear plug person, but you might be. Bring your own.

- If staying at a hotel, ask for a room on the lower levels or take the stairs down to the testing room. The last thing you want is to wait for an elevator, filled with other nervous test takers.

- Get your lunch meals and breakfast ready the night before. Know what you are going to eat for breakfast and lunch, at least the first day. Make sure you have enough food to cook and eat.

4) Energy preparation

1. Warm up the morning of your exam

Physical warm up

It is a good idea to be physically warmed up before you go to the test center. Getting the blood flow gets the mind and body thinking. You may want to do a full exercise routine. At a minimum, do a few jumping jacks, stretching exercises, take a warm shower, or go for a five-minute brisk walk.

Mental warm up

Get yourself in the zone mentally. If it is an essay day, spend ten minutes reading through a practice essay and do a brief outline. Do not worry if you do not get it right, and do not even look at the sample answer. You are not doing this to learn more stuff, but rather warm up and get yourself in the zone. On MBE day, spend a few minutes and do about 5 MBE questions. Again, no looking at the answer. You are just warming up and getting in-sync.

Energy warm up

You need good energy to spend the next six to eight hours sitting in a room and taking a mentally invigorating test. Make absolutely sure you have a good breakfast. Starbucks and a muffin do not count. Some combination of the following could work: eggs, toast, water, banana, apple, etc.

At lunch, eat a good meal. Do not mix carbs and meat together! That means no big burgers and fries at lunch. Or you might fall asleep in the afternoon, especially during a 3-hour mundane MBE or Performance test.

Eat salad with chicken and some fruit. Drink plenty of water (but not too much, where you will have to make frequent trips to the restroom). At lunch, take a walk around the neighborhood. If you can get some fresh air and disengage from the surroundings for a little bit, you will also avoid nervous people who want to talk about the exam.

Most test centers do not allow snacks into the test room. Bring a few in a plastic bag you can leave outside. They should be items like carrots, green oat bars, bananas, unsalted almonds and other healthy food you can have before you head into the test center.

12 other bar exam week rules to follow:

1. Do Your Best

We can only do the best we can with the knowledge and preparation we have at the time, right? Go there and resolve to do your best. Put faith and trust in yourself and your preparation. Know you have done the best you can to get to this point. You may hit road bumps, but that is ok. Trust in your prep.

Forget about passing or failing. Resolve to do well, write well, and give it your best. The more focused you are on the actions required and less on the outcome, the better off you will be.

2. Do not talk to other people about the exam

There is really no point in doing this on exam day. I have not heard of anyone who felt better after doing this, unless they were feeling better at another's expense. You cannot change what you wrote, and in all likelihood you will feel worse.

The ones who walk around talking about what issues they spotted are the ones who are scared they missed something and want you to be scared too! If you tell them you missed something that they got, they feel good because they think they have one less person to compete against. Do yourself and others a favor by not talking about the exam you just took.

3. In fact, do not talk to anyone

I am normally an outgoing friendly person, but not on the bar exam. I am there for one specific purpose – to take it and pass it. I do not want anyone else riling things up in my brain that I do not want there. I was very selective about who I hung out with and what I allowed into my brain during bar week. You put in way too much time to get here. If someone tries to talk to you, just smile and excuse yourself to the bathroom. If you just came from the bathroom, go to the drinking fountain.

This also means eating away from everyone else or finding a quiet corner in a restaurant. I spent the first two days eating in my car listening to music. The third day I ventured into the corner of a local restaurant.

If you are going to talk to your friends, just say hi and nod your head. Do not say anything about the exam. Do not worry. They will still be your friends afterwards.

4. Keep a level head regardless of what happens

Whatever you do, just stay focused on the task at hand. There may be all sorts of unexpected things that try to trip you up. You might be like my roommate, who was the only person sitting under a freezing air conditioner, while everyone else was nice and warm. You might have the person sitting next to you start typing right away when the essay begins without outlining, causing you to wonder if he is doing it right and you are not. You might have your psychological state messed with by a two-time repeater telling you how hard it is to pass, before you begin, as it happened to me.

These things can be part of the test. The only significance they have is that which you give it. Just allow it help you focus even more. Mentally visualizing yourself going through the week in a peaceful and calm manner will go a long way towards helping you out.

5. No more than 1 hour per essay

The bar exam is a little different than practice. Now you have three hours to spend on three essays. Even for those who were very disciplined during their practice, it can be very tempting to spend more than an hour on the first essay.

If you absolutely must, spend five minutes extra, but no more than that. Instead, move on to the next essay. If you find that you finish the next essay early and cannot spot anything else to talk about using the methods I wrote about earlier in the book, then go back and add to the first essay. Some people have scored 80's on their first essay and 0 on their last one. Do not be one of them.

6. Do not be that guy

You know, the guy who is frantically looking over rules and notes five minutes before the test center room opens. Unfortunately for me, I was that guy in law school.

But, I resolved not to be him on the bar exam. Make the bar exam different. You are not going to pick up anything of relevance those last few minutes, so do not panic yourself more by doing so. Resolve to be on top of your game and prepared ahead of time.

7. Stop studying at least one day before the exam

Energy comes in cycles, and it is important to be in a good state of energy so you can peak during your actual bar exam test days. A nice break the day before will help you refresh and charge up for the next few days. Doing last-minute practice probably will not help you that much.

I stopped my intense studying the Sunday before my Tuesday bar exam date. I did some very light attack sheet reviewing up until Monday noon the day before the exam. After that, I was done.

8. Sleep well the night before

This can easier said than done. Use the sleep techniques I described in Step 2. If nothing else, get my "Bar exam sleep" mp3 by going to http://IPassedMyBarExam.com/TheSevenSteps. It is absolutely free!

9. Watch your favorite movie the night before

There is nothing quite like watching the inspiration of Gladiator the night before I take the bar exam. After all, if Maximus can battle the entire political force of Rome and win, certainly I can take a measly bar exam, right?

10. Keep energized for Day 3

For those of you with Day 3 bar exams, know that historically, scores tend to drop off on Day 3. It is not because the material is harder. It is because people do not manage their energy well. They either get physically tired or mentally uninspired.

Do not let this happen to you. Are you really going to throw away two months of hard work and wait another three months simply because you got tired for a few hours and did not manage your energy?

Mentally activate your mind, get enough sleep, eat right, and have enough pride to take care of yourself. You are worth it and deserve it. All you have to do is focus, manage your energy, and resolve not to allow yourself to drop off. Be committed to your success.

11. Celebrate after you are done

Regardless of how it went, it is time to celebrate! Reward yourself for sticking with it, spending the two months to prepare for and take that exam. It is one of the most challenging tests you will take, and only a few people in this entire world get to this point. You are truly worthy. Celebrate and reward your efforts.

12. Do not give up, no matter what

It is really silly that some people actually quit during the bar exam. If you take it, the worst that can happen is you fail. If you quit, then you are proactively bringing about your worst case scenario and not giving yourself a chance. Quitters never prosper, and, mathematically, you cannot prosper if you quit.

What is even sillier is when those who left after the first day get their scores back and see that they actually passed their Day 1. I bet they feel great now. This has happened a surprising number of times.

No one feels like they nailed the bar exam. No one is certain they passed. Even 5-time Witkin winners get nervous about the exam and results. They key is to keep going no matter what. Whatever happened, happened. Leave it behind.

For me, when I was taking practice essays, I would usually finish them in an hour if I got everything correct. Towards the end of my practice, I was actually doing very well and consistently spending about an hour.

On Day 1, I completed my second and third essays in about 35 minutes each. That was a huge red flag to me, and I knew I missed a lot. I used the techniques I described in this book and moved forward. On Day 3, the same thing happened with two more essays, one of which I completely made up.

On my Day 2 MBE, there was a period of about 40 minutes where I completely blanked. I cannot definitively say why I did, but I just felt like I was completely out of touch with the questions and had no confidence I was getting any of them right. That was about 25 questions of blindness, which was enough to break me!

Guess what, even though it certainly did not go perfect, I passed. And you can too if you practice the techniques in this book and move forward.

And the bar student logged on to his computer the day of his results. He nervously entered his login information and immediately a screen popped up reading the following statement:

"This name appears on the pass list"

The 7 Steps to Bar Exam Success

Questions for the Author?

I would love to entertain your questions and hear your thoughts on the bar exam in general. Email me at *Dustin@IPassedMyBarExam.com*.

Want to get the Free Bar exam tips and suggestions?

Go to http://IPassedMyBarExam.com/TheSevenSteps and I will send you:

- Bar/Bri Bonus Chapter: Bar/Bri MBE secrets revealed
  - Quick tips from my Bar/Bri notes about the bar exam
  - What topics show up the most on bar exam day
  - What to focus on so you will be most prepared
- The 1-page Bar Exam Script
- Bar Exam Affirmation list
- Bar Exam sleep mp3
- Free Quick tips throughout your bar exam

Get the Bar Exam Passer's Mindset!

Build your confidence, decrease your anxiety, and transform your subconscious mind into a bar exam passer by going to http://IPassedMyBarExam/BarExamMentalEdge

Connect with us on Facebook, Twitter, Itunes, and Youtube

Facebook: http://IPassedMyBarExam.com/Facebook
Twitter: http://IPassedMyBarExam.com/Twitter
@ipassedmybarexa
YouTube: http://IPassedMyBarExam.com/Youtube
Itunes: http://IPassedMyBarExam.com/Podcasts

One more thing...

If you believe your friends or other bar exam takers would get something valuable out of this book, I would be grateful and honored if you would post and share your thoughts on your social media accounts.

And if you feel particularly strong about the contributions this made to your bar exam prep period, I would be eternally grateful if you posted a review on Amazon. Just go here and it will take you directly to the page:
http://IPassedMyBarExam.com/KindleReview

Final thoughts

Only the person who continues to move through the tunnel has the chance of seeing the light. No goal is worthwhile without a good challenge required to obtain it. This book is dedicated to all those who take the journey to help them become contributors to the greatest and most prestigious profession in the history of the world.

You can do it if you think you can, plan your mindset and tactical strategy, and take consistent action towards your success. May your journey be a blessed one.

All the Best
Dustin

Made in the USA
Lexington, KY
03 April 2014